To Carol,
god bless
you ...

Blue:
Little Cat Come Home to Stay

Carol Johnson
2830 Parkland Place
Blind Bay, BC V0E 1H1
(250) 675-3504

the One through Whom all things are possible

and to my husband, Jim, without whom I'd
know neither love nor animals.

Blue:
Little Cat Come Home to Stay

A novel by Donna Richards

Illustrated by Jesse Gentes

Borealis Press
Ottawa, Canada
2000

Canada

We acknowledge the financial support of the Government of Canada through the Book Publishing Industry Development Program (BPIDP), the Canada Council and the Ontario Arts Council, for our publishing activities.

Canadian Cataloguing in Publication Data

Richards, Donna Jean, 1949 -
      Blue: little cat come home to stay

ISBN 0-88887-160-0 (bound) - ISBN 0-88887-162-7 (pbk.)

      I. Cats - Juvenile fiction. 1. Title.

PS8585.I1735B58 2000   jC813'.6   C00-900123-9
PZ7.R3788BI 2000

Printed and bound in Canada on acid free paper.

Contents

Blue Visits 1
Blue Helps With The Wood 5
Blue's Dark Barn 9
Last Night In The Dark Barn .13
Blue Has To Choose 17
Blue Is Needed 19
New Home 25
New Chores 29
The Barn Chores 33
Noon Nap 39
Evening Chores 41
A Night Inside 47
Pastures And A Problem 51
Blue Is Puzzled 55
Blue Sets Out 59
Blue Finds The Solution 63
Blue Brings The Solution Home 67
Cleaned Up 71
Fed 75
Good Morning 79
A Bath 85
To Stay 91

CHAPTER ONE

Blue Visits

'I'd better warn her I'm coming,' thought the little, grey, tabby cat, meowing several times as he trotted through the narrow forest between the two old farms. He used his most sorrowful, little meow, repeating it several times with only the shortest pause in between. Sure enough, the old woman looked up from her work in the barn just as he paused to look in either direction at the edge of the trees.

"C'mon then, Blue," she said, leaning the broom against the wall of the stall and squatting down to stroke the little cat and talk to him when he crossed the paddock and strode into the barn. "Where have you been? I haven't seen you for several days. You must be hungry. Come and we'll get some kibbles for you."

'Ah, this is so nice,' thought the little cat as he arched his back and rubbed against her legs. 'She's such a nice soft thing, and so generous with the kibbles. I hope she'll get some milk, too.' He felt so good that he rolled over and squirmed about on his back, stretching his paws out and rolling from side to side. He began to purr as she bent over to scratch his tummy for a while.

"I see we'll have to get the brush out after you've eaten. Look at this mess on your belly. Where have you been, funny old Blue?"

His only response was to purr louder and faster and nudge a little closer to her; he never could get enough of the feel and smell of her. It went well with the quiet and calm of this old place. The barn was always clean and bright and, during the day, was empty. The horses were way out in the pasture, quietly grazing, and everything here was still and calm. He liked the sweet smell of hay in the feed room and up in the loft too. Even as he purred and rubbed, he looked longingly up at the soft hay in the loft. He really was tired.

Seeing his look, the old woman straightened up and took his saucers down from their shelf. She opened the container with the blue lid and filled one saucer with nice kibbles, then put it on the table under the window. "Up you come, then, old fella; you look tired but you'd better eat first. Do you want a bit of milk too?" she asked as he settled down on his haunches and began to crunch the kibbles. He turned his head slightly so he could look into her eye and let her know he'd love some milk, before settling right into his meal. "Okay," she said, "you eat up while I go into the house and get you some milk. Want it warm?" Again he turned enough to look deeply into her eyes, conveying his consent, before returning to his food.

When she returned with the other saucer full of warmed milk, he was almost finished the kibbles. He crunched up the last couple and paused to wipe his whiskers before rubbing against her arm and settling in to lap up the milk. Oh, it was so good. What a nice old lady. He liked her grey hair, especially when her braid fell down in front of her and he could play with it a little, and he felt especially good and safe when he rubbed against her wrinkled cheek and when she ran her soft hand the length of his back and up to the tip of his tail. When she bent her slightly gnarled fingers to scratch him behind his ears, he couldn't stop the purr from exploding inside him. Life was so good here!

Finishing his milk, he stepped up onto the window sill and began to wash his face. "Ah, you're done, are you?" she said, reaching for his little brush and plucking him off the sill. "We'd better give you a tidy-up before you settle down for your nap."

He couldn't even wonder what he was keeping her from, so happy was he to be held on her lap while she brushed his coat and chattered to him. "Some of the shine is gone from your coat, Blue. You really should watch what you eat, you know. And why must you get yourself so tired? Look here, there's a little nip out of your ear. Have you been fighting again? Silly fella, one day you'll meet a cat that will really whip you, you know, and then what will I do? It's all very well to have the horses and the old dog, but who will sit on my lap if you lose a fight? And who will sit by the wood pile and watch me chop the wood? It's getting to be hard work for me, you know, and I need you to sit and keep me going. You'd better be more careful."

In response he purred a little louder and rubbed more closely into the curve of her tummy. It was really so warm and comfy there, he didn't know why he couldn't just stay and stay and stay. He folded his front paws, one over the other, and began to settle for a nap. Life was so very good. They sat quietly for a while, hearing only the sounds of birds in the fields and the occasional distant snort from one of the grazing horses. After a while, she stirred saying, "I'll have to finish these chores, old fella. Where are you going to sleep today?"

In response, he stretched, arching his back fully and rubbing her chin with it as he did, and then hopped onto the table, crouched and leapt onto the beam and stepped into the loft. His little bed was still there, a carefully flattened circle in the fresh hay. With a little sigh of contentment, he curled around, carefully wrapping his tail as far around him as it would reach, closed his eyes and drifted to sleep. Below him the old woman retrieved her broom and finished sweeping out the alley of the barn. For a while she puttered around, cleaning the horses' feed troughs and tidying some of the shelves, before she quietly said, "Have a good sleep, Blue; I hope I see you later" and left the barn, her morning chores done.

Inside the house, she made herself some tea and prepared to sit a spell. She thought about how much nicer the days were when Blue came and she could spend a little time with him and talk to him. He was such a nice little cat, so comfortable and friendly. He had such a marvelous purr, like a kettle boiling within his chest, and he always seemed so happy and carefree. Yet he loved and gave a great deal. 'Life is good when there is a cat to cuddle' she thought, as she gazed out the window. 'Mostly life is good anyway, even if it takes me longer and longer to do the chores, but it is just extra good when Blue is around.'

CHAPTER TWO

Blue Helps With The Wood

After her tea and her rest, she had to go back outside to chop the wood, one chore that was getting ever harder for her. Outside, the old dog got up from his place between the path and the verandah and waddled over to her, tail wagging in its huge arc. "Hello, old man. Coming to check if I'm okay, are you? Well, I am. How about you?" She scratched his head, giving extra attention to the place that he liked so much just behind his right ear. After sixteen years, she knew exactly what pleased him the most. "I'm off to cut some wood, old boy, so you needn't worry. Just lie back down and continue your sleep. Won't be long now before you don't wake up at all. You be quiet this afternoon, though; little Blue is here today and he likes it quiet, you know."

Satisfied that she was fine, the old dog turned around and eased himself down to continue his nap, glad that the day was warm and soothing for his old bones and muscles. He liked his warm spot and only moved to his other place on the verandah beside the back door when the weather was really wet and cold.

The old woman went to the woodshed, a lean-to attached to the side of the barn. Carefully she counted out the rounds that she would need to chop for the day and then added one more to the pile, smiling to herself as she did so. How many years, now, had she been adding the one extra piece, the one meant to serve her in case of an emergency? Had it already been eleven years since Josiah had lain down one afternoon and not wakened from his nap? That's a long time to chop one extra round every day. Maybe, since she was tired, she could skip one day. No, better save such a treat for a day when she really couldn't chop. Wood lined up, she took the axe with the special handle that Josiah had made for her, "just in case of an emergency,' he had said, and took a deep breath before beginning.

Out of habit, she glanced over her shoulder to the block standing just inside the shed at the right of the doorway. A smile broke across her face as she saw Blue hop up onto the block and take his place there, back in the sun, face turned toward her as if to say, 'go ahead, old woman, you can do it. I'll sit here and keep count.' With an ease she hadn't felt earlier, she raised the axe and let it fall, swiftly splitting the round in two. Good thing she had spent all that time when she was young watching her father chop wood; she had noticed then that you let the tools work for you instead of struggling against them. If you could raise the axe properly and aim it accurately, the force of the fall of the axe was enough to split any good wood. Taking the time to keep the axe sharp was all it took. Still, at her age, the axe was itself beginning to feel heavy and she had to carry the wood just a few pieces at a time, making more trips from the woodshed to the wood box on the back porch than she used to even a couple of years ago. Oh well, today she had Blue to help.

And there he sat, his head following the swing of the axe. Of course, his head didn't have to move very quickly any more, but he didn't seem to mind. She knew he would stay until she was finished. He always did when he was home. When she was half done, she went over to the doorway; Blue stood up and moved to the edge of the block, making room for her to sit down.

"Good old Blue," she said, with a slight sigh as she pulled her work gloves off and laid them down on the ground beside her, "you're a pretty patient puss, aren't you?" Happily and gently, he climbed onto her lap and moved about looking for a comfortable position. She reached out and tucked his back legs beneath him, helping him to settle into the crook of her arm as she began to scratch behind his ears. Instantly, the purr began. In delight his eyes half shut, though he kept his head tipped up toward her face. Gently she bent her head down and rubbed her cheek against his head. As she did so, her braid fell forward, and he reached out one cupped paw and batted it from side to side.

"Ah, Blue," she said, "wouldn't it be grand if we could just sit here forever? But you know, if I don't get the wood cut, I won't have a fire, and if I don't have a fire, I won't be warm and won't be able to cook supper. Besides, I won't have a way to heat your milk, you know, so we'd better get on with it. Just a few more minutes rest and we'll finish the job."

Quietly they sat in the sun, each one content, each one secure, each one simply living the moment. When she reached down to pick up her gloves, Blue moved to the side, willing to let her get on with the work. He resumed his position, sitting upright, watching every fall of the axe, seeing the pile of split wood grow.

"Almost there, Blue," she said, "only the extra piece left and then we're done." The axe fell, the wood split and a look of triumph crossed her face. Blue hopped down from the block and trotted over to rub against her legs. "We did it again, old fella, got the chores done ourselves," she said as she stooped to stroke his arched back. Oh, it was such a happy moment. He followed her as she returned the axe to its hook on the wall, and followed her back as she returned to the new pile of wood. Each time she bent to pick up three pieces of wood, Blue rubbed against her, and each time she walked over to the house, he followed behind her, careful to walk around the old dog, who watched steadily from one eye, but didn't bother to move.

Back to the woodshed they'd go, and again he'd rub against her as she bent to pick up the wood. Back and forth, back and forth, until the wood box was full and only the extra pieces remained in the new pile of wood. Blue rubbed against her as she picked these up and then stepped to the side to let her go past him to the back of the shed. He followed her and watched her place the extra pieces on the emergency pile. She was right; it had grown large, and that felt good. Blue scrambled up to the top of it and, as she always did, she scooped him into her arms for a hug and a rub against her cheek. Their work was done.

"Want a treat then, little puss?" she asked, carrying him around into the barn. He caught her eye and began to purr loudly, trying to burrow closer to her as she held him. "You're a good old counter, aren't you, fella? You always know when we're done. Come on, then, sit on the table while I get your treat." And there he sat, head tipped slightly to one side, ears erect, eyes slightly squinted and shining. From the jar up on the shelf, she took a few cat treats and held them out to him. He bent his head into her outstretched hand and quickly munched up the tasty treats, finishing with a lick of his lips and a flick of his whiskers. Then he sat back and carefully cleaned his face, using his right paw as he always did.

"I'm in for my rest, then, before time to let the horses in and give them their oats," she said. "What about you?" In answer, he stretched out in the sunny spot on the shelf near the window and carefully began licking his front legs. "Okay," she said, "you have your bath. I'll see you later. Be a good puss, now." And she walked over to the house for her rest and her dinner.

CHAPTER THREE

BLUE'S DARK BARN

After finishing his bath, the little cat sat and looked around for a while. It was really a very nice place to live and she was the nicest of people. He'd like to stay and stay and stay. If only this silliness would go from inside of him. He began to pace back and forth on the shelf, looking this way and that. Finally, he jumped down and began looking all around the barn, sniffing in all the corners, snooping all about. His little tail flicked from side to side and his pace quickened as he roamed about the barn. He looked out the door into the paddock and the trees, shook his head and returned to his pacing. Always, though, he returned to that door. He wasn't tired. He wasn't hungry. But he wasn't comfortable any more either. He paced back and forth in the doorway, back and forth, back and forth. Finally with one sad look over his shoulder, he ran out the door, across the paddock and into the trees. At the far edge of the forest he sat for several minutes.

'I'll try to sneak by him,' he thought, as, crouched low to the ground, he inched his way across the field toward the old, dark barn on the other side of the pasture. He could see the man swinging the huge scythe and his two sons raking the hay and scooping it up into the wagon. He hoped they were too busy to notice him. To his left he could see the dog, and he hoped the man had told him to stay. Stupid dog always did what he was told, so if the man had ordered him, the little cat knew he didn't have to worry. He couldn't see the other dog anywhere, but he didn't have to worry about her; she was a friend. Slowly, he crept on, his eyes moving from man to dog and back as he moved determinedly toward the barn. At the sound of the wagon rattling and creaking as the men moved it closer to their work, the little cat hunkered even closer to the ground and froze. He was as still as an old log until the sound ceased and the men returned to their work. 'The noises over here are really frightful,' he thought, but he resumed his sneaking toward the barn. Suddenly,

9

the sound of the swinging scythe stopped and the voice of the man rang out across the field; "well, look who is trying to sneak his way back to the barn again. It's old Tiger back from his tom-catting again."

Caught, the little cat would just have to play this thing out, so he began to meow, short, sharp, demanding meows, as he redirected his path to walk toward the man. He didn't look directly at the man; just walked toward him, scolding him with the sounds the man didn't like. When he got close to the man, the little cat just sat down and continued to scold.

"Cheeky as ever," the man said, "you're a rum one, Tiger. And you're in the way as always, too. Go on; get outa here. Clear out. We've work to do here. You'll not get a scrap from us. You can earn your keep. There's plenty of mice around here. Now git!" he yelled as he waved his arm angrily in the air.

Just as the little cat turned to trot toward the barn leaving the man to his work, he heard the low growl of the dog and sensed the danger. He broke into a run when the dog barked and leapt toward him. Across the field they ran, huge dog loping after the small cat, both animals with their ears flat against their heads, the cat running and bounding in leaps that seemed larger than any small animal could manage. With heart racing and eyes wide, the little cat reached the barn just steps ahead of the dog and scrambled up the support pole to the rafters, far above the dog's reach. Curling on his haunches, he smirked down at the panting dog, eyes wide and tale flicking from side to side. The dog let out a few growls and a feeble woof or two before turning and trotting back out to the field. After a few minutes, the little cat settled himself more comfortably on the rafter to watch and wait a while.

This barn was so dark and so dank. There certainly were mice to be had; the place was alive with them, even smelled more of mice than of sweet hay. But then this was a cow barn and it was seldom cleaned out. The rough men who had this farm did only what they had to and nothing more. If they were tired or lazy, they sometimes didn't let the cows out for a day or two and then they just kind of shoveled the worst of the manure out the door after them. The corners were pretty well packed with old manure. The little cat thought that if it weren't for the milking that had to be done, the men probably wouldn't let the cows in at all. He was glad of the milking, for the men were so sloppy that he got to lick up the spilt milk. That was the closest he got to a treat at this place. As he sat up on the rafter, he wondered why he always came back at all.

Of course, he'd been born here so this was home, even if he didn't like it much. He was just one of many cats here. Every once in a while, the man came into the barn, climbed the ladder to the loft and scooped up new litters of kittens and took them to the creek and drowned them, but some of the mother cats were clever enough to hide their litters well, so there were always plenty of cats. The going was pretty rough sometimes, especially at night when the fights broke out. He was one of the smallest cats, but he had learned to defend himself a little and to run and hide to avoid the whole mess. He just wasn't a born fighter and he saw no reason to become one.

He sensed that the men wouldn't really approve of such behaviour from what they called "Tiger the tomcat" but he couldn't do anything about that. Besides, they didn't know what went on in the barn or on the farm at night. They were always too rowdy or too sleepy to respond to any noises or scuffles at all. They didn't even stir themselves when the cows cried out. One had bawled and bawled all night long once when she'd got caught beneath a broken plank, but no one came to help her. By morning, the hide was torn all across her neck and back where she'd struggled to get free. The man had responded only in anger at her decreased value and not given any love at all. He set her free, yelling and cussing at her the whole time. The little cat seemed to scowl as he remembered her suffering and the man's coldness. This was a hard home indeed, but home it was. Funny, the little old lady next door thought hers was his home, but he'd been born here in this dark barn, so he supposed he must return here several times a week.

CHAPTER FOUR

LAST NIGHT IN THE DARK BARN

He decided to stay up on the rafter for a while, perhaps even for the night. He had no desire to find the other cats and nobody wanted or needed him here. He didn't need to go after mice this night, for his tummy was full. Perhaps he'd be left alone here; if he got comfortable and sat real still, maybe no one would notice him. He reached his front paws as far out ahead of him as they would go; then, digging his claws into the rough wood of the rafter, he stretched as hard as he could, kneading his claws rapidly as he did so. He ended by arching his back way up, almost into a point at the top, then stretched each hind leg in turn out behind him. Then he settled on the rafter, front paws folded neatly, one covering the other, his tail carefully tucked in beside his left haunch. The position was good; he could see the doorway as well as the depths of the barn from here. He'd be quick to see any danger if it came. There he sat, eyes blinking occasionally, head nodding from time to time.

He was a patient cat, could sit for hours and hours, focussed on his present task. It didn't seem long before it grew dusky and he heard the cows moving toward the barn door. Soon the men would come to let them in and milk them. He crouched a little lower and fixed his head on the doorway so he wouldn't have to move a muscle when they came. He heard other cats scurrying to the dark corners of the loft. None chose to be around when the rough men had to work in the barn. Sure enough, the young men clumped through the door and began throwing small bits of hay into the mangers that ran down either side of the barn alley, complaining and cussing as they did their bit of work. The old man opened the gate that separated the pastures from the barn, and the cows pushed toward the barn, mooing and bawling in their discomfort. In their eagerness to be milked, they shoved through the doorway and pushed each other about, each trying to get to the front of the long line and be milked first. The noise got louder and louder, each sound edged with impatience and discomfort, and the little cat began to wish he had gone somewhere else.

Soon, to the cattle noises were added the scraping of the milking stools, the clank of the metal milk pails and the ringing and foaming of milk filling the pails. Occasionally, the men groaned as they finished one cow and moved to the next. They didn't seem to enjoy this task, but at least they were too busy to do much swearing or complaining. Only when a cow moved or kicked, did a burst of cursing explode across the barn.

It didn't take long for the barn to warm up with the rows of cows down there, and before long the smells of sweat and manure rose to where the little cat sat. He wrinkled his nose and would have pulled back if he hadn't been so determined to remain unnoticed. He knew from experience, though, that it would soon be over and the men would leave. Tonight, having had his tummy filled so well earlier, he wouldn't have to go down and scrap with the other cats and the black dog for the spilt milk, so he could relax and watch.

Sure enough, the men soon emptied the last of their pails into the large milk cans on the wagon and, tossing the empty pails into their corner, left the barn with the wagon. In better kept barns, of course, the milk pails would have been carefully washed and the cats would have had much less to lap up, but here the cats benefitted from the carelessness of the men. The little cat watched as the other cats emerged from their hiding places and began to scramble among the milk pails and around the space where the wagon had been; a lot had been spilled there, too. A few quick spats broke out; as usual, the large, white, mother cat knocked most of the others out of her way. The little cat was pleased to see the black dog find a good spill part way down the alley and lap that up herself. She had a rough go of it amongst all these hungry cats. He saw, too, that she'd caught something to eat earlier in the day; she checked the pile of bones for any morsels she might have left before going back outside. The little cat thought he could rest okay now that he'd seen that she was alright, and he'd been successful; nobody had noticed him perched high above everything.

So he tried to settle down for the night. Below him the cows rested, more content now, more quiet. The chewing sound would continue through the night, but it was a comfortable sound. Occasionally there would be some complaining, for even the cows were not fed enough, but the night would be much quieter than the evening.

CHAPTER FIVE

BLUE HAS TO CHOOSE

He had some trouble settling himself and remained with eyes wide for a long time. Several times he tried to sleep, but something deep inside him would not rest. In the darkest part of the night, he found himself having to give up the safety of stillness and pace back and forth across the old rafter. Back and forth he went, and he was confused, for he didn't usually feel like this here at home. He was used to not liking it, but he wasn't used to being stirred by restlessness here. And yet he could not settle down. Back and forth he went.

He strained and strained his ears, trying to determine what might be calling him, but he heard nothing. It was a very still and dark night. He moved along another rafter and sat above the doorway, straining all his attention out into the night. Soon, he paid no attention to the barn activity at all, hearing and feeling only the still, darkness outside. His whole being seemed drawn to the forest, a place he didn't like at night. He shook his head; no sense going into the woods at night. There were too many big raccoons in there; it was a foolish place for a small cat to go. And yet he couldn't shake off this yearning he had. Eyes wide, he sat on the beam above the door, wary, but unsettled. He was going to have to choose. Soon he knew he'd have to go, raccoons or no raccoons.

The journey across the pasture was quick and without event. He crouched down in the high grasses at the edge of the woods and was perfectly still, watching and listening. The woods were dark, even darker than the pasture on this moonless night. He'd have to watch for large owls, too, especially if he stayed in the tall grass. Before long, one might spot him. He had to go on. Staying close to the ground, he eased out of the grass and slunk into the forest. Eyes wide, whiskers twitching and hair standing up along his back, he moved quickly through the woods, pausing only when he sensed he was being watched. A sudden noise to his right sent him running the rest of the way and up onto the paddock fence at the forest's edge.

His tail flicked frantically from side to side as he sat on the post, looking all around him. Everything was dark, the barn all shut up. He'd never come here at night before but he knew he had to come now. He also knew he needed a safe place, so he ran around to the woodshed and hid in the farthest corner of the emergency pile. There he hunched down and waited, trying to calm down. Funny, he didn't feel safe here as he usually did, but he had no desire or notion to go back either. Something was wrong. He remained crouched and still, waiting to know what to do. Deep inside him, the restlessness welled up, worse than ever before. It almost hurt him, so strong it was. And it grew and grew. Still he waited. Still it grew until it threatened to burst inside him.

Then, he knew. He knew exactly what to do. The fierce restlessness burst like a huge bubble, releasing the little cat from his crouched position. His choice was made. He sat up, gave his face a little wash and tidied up his fur a little. Then, in the dark of the night, he hopped down from the wood pile and trotted confidently out into the cool air. He followed the path to the little old lady's house, trotting steadily toward the back verandah. He stopped beside the form of the big old dog. It was absolutely still in the night. No eye opened to watch him pass. No muscle moved. No tail twitched. Old Rex wouldn't feel his old joints hurting in the morning. The little cat kept silent a while, paying tribute to the kind old fellow Rex had been, then resumed his trot and ran up the back steps.

'I'd better warn her I'm coming,' he thought, as he began his sorrowful meowing. 'No,' he thought, 'I'd better call her and tell her I'm home.' And with that he began a new meowing, a pleasant calling, halfway between the sorrowful cry he had once used to call her and the demanding call he'd used for the rough man. Patiently, Blue sat down by the door and called his old woman, his firm but gentle meow singing in the night.

CHAPTER SIX

BLUE IS NEEDED

Though it was dark and very late, the old woman hadn't been able to sleep well. Restlessly, she had dozed on and off through the night. Dimly, she heard a cat calling. At first she thought it was Blue, but then the sound changed to one she hadn't heard before. 'Silly old fool,' she thought, 'you're letting your wishes run away with you. Blue has never come at night and has never come to the door. Besides, Old Rex would have barked if anything were here. Just get yourself off to sleep and stop imagining things.' She rolled over thinking that changing her position would help her sleep. But the meowing persisted. It was really a very pretty sound, very friendly, very gentle, but very persistent. Well, it wouldn't hurt to get up and look. She was awake anyway.

She swung her legs over the side of the bed and slid her feet into her well-worn carpet slippers. They hadn't been slip-ons when they were new, but over the years she had worn them in so they slipped on easily and flapped softly as she walked. She reached for her soft, terry-robe and slipped it on over her thick flannel night gown. 'No sense getting chilled,' she thought. As she walked from the bedroom to the kitchen, she could hear the cat more clearly, and the sound was coming from the back door. She lit the lamp before opening the door.

"Blue," she cried, stooping to rub her hand across his back, "it is you! What are you doing here at this time of night and here in the doorway? And why didn't Old Rex warn me you were coming?" Though the little cat longed to rub against her ankles, in response he sat down and stared deep into her eyes, meowing gently and a little sadly. He was very firm as he looked into the depths of her soul. He had two messages for her and he must convey them clearly, the good before the bad. So he sat patiently, looking and looking, occasionally meowing kindly.

"It's chilly, Blue," she said, "we can't stand out here. Do you

19

want to come in and tell me about it?"

'Good,' he thought, 'this will be better for her.' So he got up and rubbed against her ankles, a little purr escaping despite his resolve to do business before pleasure. With the confidence of a cat who was needed and loved, Blue stepped across the doorway of the kitchen, not at all unsettled by being inside a house for the first time in his life. Once inside, he rubbed up against her legs a few times again, then sat quietly down beside her, looking up at her as she closed the door behind him.

"Oh Blue," she said, with a few tears in her eyes, "this could only mean you've come home at last. Come on for a cuddle then, good fellow." She bent and scooped him up, carried him over to the rocker by the stove and sat down, settling him on her lap. The purr erupted again before he could do anything about it, so he gave himself up to a few moments of bliss. The old woman lifted him gently and rubbed her tear-dampened cheek against his head.

"Such a good puss," she murmured softly, "we'll have to fix up a few spots in the house for you and get some saucers in here, too. We'll leave the ones in the barn and just have some here as well. That way you can eat wherever you are. Perhaps I'll get another brush, too, one for here and one for the barn. Can't have you getting all shabby, you know. Tomorrow evening I'll begin to knit a small blanket for you; you'll need a spot of your own here. It will be just grand, Blue, you'll see."

And with that she rubbed her soft cheek back and forth against his ear, just the way he liked it. Warmly and securely, the two sat in the rocker for a long time. The only sounds around were the gentle roll of the rockers against the floor and the rolling purr of the little cat as he nestled on the good woman's lap. She understood his first message, that he was here to stay, and together they rested in the peace of being settled.

As the grey dawn began to erase the dark of night, Blue knew he must get on with business. Oh it was difficult to tear himself away from the comfort of their rest, but he must. So, he squirmed a little against her clasp, just enough to let her know he wanted to choose the position now. He didn't hop down to the floor, but moved himself out to the very edge of her lap and sat facing her, looking straight into her eyes. Now that she knew he was hers, he must convey the second message. He focussed all his attention as he gazed and gazed at her. Then he began to cry, short, quiet little cries of sadness.

"What is it, little fella?" she asked, "what troubles you? Are you hungry?"

Quickly he laid one paw on her hand, as if to say, 'no, that's not it; you needn't get food,' and cried a little more.

"I didn't think that sounded like your hungry cry," she said. "It must be something else. Do you want to go out?"

No, he didn't want to go out, but he must. And he must take her with him. He took a quick look around the kitchen. Spying her coat hanging on its hook near the door, he hopped down from her lap and went and sat beneath it, meowing as he looked up at it.

"Funny old Blue," she said. "You don't need me to take you out. You know your way around here and you're safe here. Don't be silly." But the little cat remained beneath the coat, meowing persistently. As she watched him and wondered, the little old woman felt a small grip of fear tug at her heart. Why would the little cat want her to go out with him? The cat's plaintive meowing reminded her that she had wondered why she hadn't heard Old Rex warn her of Blue's arrival in the dark of night, and she shivered, though she wasn't cold. Could it be that Rex needed help and the little cat was trying to tell her? 'No,' she thought, 'it wouldn't be that or he'd have demanded I go much sooner. It must be that he's just not used to the house yet." With that thought, she began to rock once again.

Seeing that she wasn't understanding him, Blue ran back to her and rubbed three times against her legs, then returned to cry beneath the coat. When she didn't respond, he ran back and rubbed against her again, before quickly returning to his place below the coat. He cried a little louder as she sat there, then looked hard at the woman, yearning with all his heart that she would get up. He had to do this thing.

"Okay, little fella," she said, getting up from the chair, "I'll come outside, but this had better not be the beginning of your demanding I come out every time you need to go." As she lifted the coat from the hook and put it on, Blue rubbed back and forth against her ankles, moving aside only to let her trade her slippers for the shoes on the mat beside the door. As she opened the door and stepped out, he was right at her side. "Silly cat," she said, "I expected you to run ahead, you were so insistent." He stayed at her side, meowing sadly.

"Okay, we'll go down the steps," she said, as she moved across the verandah. Suddenly she stopped and the little cat immediately rubbed back and forth, back and forth against her legs. "Rex," she cried, "why don't you greet me?" As a small sob escaped from her throat, the little cat rubbed harder, even going between her legs and rubbing against both ankles at once. He meowed a little louder and quickly moved out of her way as she moved toward the stairs. He didn't want to trip her, so he stayed just to her side, continuing his meowing, hoping she would hear him and feel a little better.

She reached the still form of the old dog and knelt beside him, tears running down her cheeks now. "Oh Rex," she said, "I knew it would soon be time and I know it will be better for you. You won't hurt any more now, won't feel the cold and struggle so hard to look after me even though you were so tired, but oh, how I'll miss you. You were such a faithful fellow and so kind. Whatever will I do alone after all these years?" As she rubbed the still head of her old friend, she cried quietly.

The little cat sat off to the side, watching and waiting for his time. When the woman's quiet crying became tinged with desperation, he got up, resumed his meowing and moved to her side, gently rubbing against her. Slowly he moved toward her outstretched arm, coming into her line of vision as she peered through her tears at the silent form of her old friend. The cat paused and turned to face her, meowing questioningly as he tried to catch her eye. Finally she noticed him, hearing his questioning meows and seeing his little up-turned face.

"Oh, Blue," she said, "you knew, didn't you? You knew I needed you. Life is so hard, sometimes, so lonely. I'm so glad you've come. I just don't know how I would carry on with no one to care for and no one to care. But you need me too, don't you? Come on, then, come sit with me."

Though the early morning was chilly, the old woman eased herself from crouching to sitting and she took the little cat on her lap. There she sat beside the still form of her long-time friend, comforted and warmed by her little cat come home to stay. They were silent for a long while, comfortable together, she having to say goodbye to Old Rex, he having to begin to settle in to his new life. The little cat nestled more deeply into her lap with a touch of relief; he had accomplished both his first tasks. From the warmth and security of his new position, vaguely he wondered what would be next.

CHAPTER SEVEN

NEW HOME

As the sun rose, chasing away the last of the pre-dawn greyness, the old woman stirred herself. "Well, little fella," she said, "we've got tasks to do now. We have to move on, you know." So saying, she gave his ears a brisk scratch and put her hands down to push herself up from the ground. Blue hopped from her lap and started for the house ahead of her, making her chuckle a little despite her sadness. "Oh, Blue," she said, "you're taking over already. What makes you think we should head for the house, you little monkey?" He paused long enough to look behind him and see that she was coming and then leapt up the verandah steps to wait for her at the door.

Inside, she said, "I've made my decision, Blue. This is one of those times when I'll just get a little help. I had the phone run in years ago just to use in emergencies, though I never bothered with the hydro, and I'm going to use that phone today. I'll call even before I get our breakfast."

She took off her coat and shoes, put her slippers back on and went over to stir up the fire and get the kettle boiling, Blue trailing along next to her leg. "You don't have to follow me everywhere," she said. "Go ahead and find a comfy spot and make yourself at home." But the little cat chose to stay at her side for a while longer.

Once the fire was fixed, she crossed to the phone on the wall and rummaged in the papers on the little shelf beneath it. Carefully, she dialed the number she had found. "It's Martha here," she said into the mouthpiece, "and I need to talk to the Vet." After a slight pause she resumed, "Yes, good morning, Doc. I need some help today. No, it's too late for you; it's your son I need. Old Rex has gone on. I've said my farewells and just need young Allan to lay him to rest down under the old apple tree. . . . Soon, if he could; the horses are needing their oats, but I'll not go outside again until he's gone."

After a long pause, she replied, "Oh thanks ever so much. I'll look for him in half an hour or so. Just tell him to help himself to the shovels in the shed. He knows the spot. God bless you both. Oh, and Doc, I've got a little puss, now; he moved in last night. Yes, it's just wonderful. Thanks again." She replaced the receiver and turned to the stove, the little cat still at her side.

"That's done, Blue. Now we just need to get things on the right track for the day. I should be dressed by now and here I am still in my night things. I'll just set the oatmeal cooking and the tea steeping and I'll dress in the time it takes for them to be ready. Guess I'll find you some saucers, too."

While the kind, old woman went to dress, Blue took the time to investigate his new house a little. Her bedroom looked good — big old bed with soft, fluffy covers, a small rocker with a padded seat and back in one corner, a tall dresser with several boxes and two lamps on top and a long, cedar chest with a padded top and many, small, knitted animals sitting upon it. There were a few pictures on the walls, and the window, with its small panes and light, lacy curtains, had a wide, wooden sill on which he was sure he could sit comfortably sometime.

The other room also had small-paned windows, three of them, two on one wall and one on another, with wide, wooden sills, and bright, clean curtains. Underneath one window was a long bench, covered with cushions and knitted animals. There were several large, comfortable chairs in here and a long sofa. A chair with rockers and a soft cushion was pulled close to the fireplace at one end and beside it stood a table with a lamp. Next to it was a basket full of bright-coloured wool and several pairs of knitting needles. That looked like it might be fun. On the end wall, stood a large, dark-wooden thing with alternating white and black strips running its length. A round stool stood in front of this and a lamp sat on its top. Each corner had a small table with a lamp and there was another low table in front of the sofa. A worn book lay open on the table. A large, oval, braided rug covered the middle of the floor.

Blue went back to the kitchen and checked the old woman. She wasn't ready yet, so he darted into the room and over to the big, dark thing and leapt onto the stool in front of it. He sniffed a little, then reached out a paw to feel the white tiles. They moved! He pulled back his paw, waited, then reached out again, a little firmer this time. A sound rang out, startling him, and he ran back to the kitchen. The old woman laughed; "You found the piano, did you, Blue? Never seen one before? Doesn't get much use now, but I'll show you a little one day. Right now it's breakfast time."

Patiently he followed her around as she got a bowl, a cup and two saucers from a cupboard and a spoon from a drawer. These she put on the table then paused. "Now where will we put your saucer?" she wondered aloud. "I know; I'll put a little mat in the corner near the table and you can have your milk there. You could sit there while I eat, too." She went into the pantry-storage room next to the back door and came back with a round, braided rug, a tiny version of the one in the living room. "Made this years ago," she said. "It's yours now."

Blue followed along beside her as she put the mat down and then turned to the huge ice chest near the sink. From behind its heavy door, she got out a pitcher of milk and a bit of butter. Putting these on the table, she turned to the stove and retrieved the teapot from the upper warming shelf and the small pot of oatmeal from the back of the stove top. Returning to the table, she placed the teapot on the braided pad next to her cup and saucer and dished the oatmeal into her bowl. Then she moved to the sink and ran water into the empty pot. Still Blue followed her, tail straight up, feet padding softly on the floor, head cocked a little to one side. At the table, she spooned a bit of butter into the middle of her oatmeal, then poured milk from the pitcher over the top. "And you, Blue?" she asked, pouring some of the rich milk into his saucer. "Come on, then," she said, as she took the saucer over to his new mat in the corner. Putting it down, she paused to give him a little scratch behind the ear before she returned to the table and sat down. She bowed her head and sat quietly for a moment before picking up her spoon and beginning.

"Have to start the day right, Blue, have a good breakfast, you know. I'm a little late this morning, but time doesn't matter that much any more. The horses will wait, and the rest won't hurt them. They're all old now, too. Not many left. I had to sell most of them when Josiah went, but I couldn't let them all go. Then later, I had to take old Jenny because no one wanted her. I couldn't let them kill her just because she was too old to breed, so I took her in. She's the grey. I got Misty the same way. She's the black. Fawn (she's the Buckskin) has always been here, must be over twenty years now, and so has Rosy, the little bay. Then there's Sarah; have you seen her? She's the little mule. I took her about five years ago because no one wanted her; they thought she was useless being too small to pack anything, so I took her. I don't think she knows she's a mule. She seems happy enough with just the horses around. That's the lot of them now, all old and happy just to have good food and a dry barn to sleep in. They're not much trouble and they deserve a home. So I keep them. Think you'll like helping me out?"

The little cat had finished his milk as she talked and was cleaning his face and paws and trying to lick his bib clean. He did have a tiny white bib beneath his chin, surrounded by the blue-grey that was really almost hidden in the bold stripes that made him tabby after all. He thought he'd understand the old mule, for he was small, too, and no one had really wanted him before. He wasn't old so might not understand that part so well, but he agreed that old age, like a small size, was no reason to abandon anyone. He hoped she'd finish her meal soon so they could get out to the barn. He looked up to see how she was doing. She had pushed her bowl back and pulled her cup and saucer closer to her, enjoying her morning tea.

Seeing Blue was finished, the gentle woman said, "I'm done except for my tea, too, so you can join me now if you want. Come on up on my lap."

With a last lick of his bib, he rose and trotted over, crouched slightly and hopped onto her lap. From here he could see out the window and he noted that the weather was good. 'Yes,' he thought, 'life will be good in this home where I am needed.'

CHAPTER EIGHT

NEW CHORES

From his spot on the old lady's knee, Blue soon noted a dusty, blue van, pulling up near the barn. The old woman heard it too. "That will be Allan," she said. "I'm glad he's come so quickly." She didn't rise, though, just sat sipping her tea and stroking Blue. "May as well enjoy my tea while Allan does his work."

More curious than she, Blue rose from her knee and stepped onto the window sill so he had a better view outside. He saw a young, sandy-haired fellow get out of the van and walk toward the house, carrying a clean, burlap sack. He paused and bent over for a moment as he came along the path by the verandah before taking the steps two at a time and rapping briskly at the back door. Blue jumped back onto the old woman's lap just as the man opened the door enough to stick his head in and say,

"Mornin' Mrs. Oaks. Don't get up; just wanted to let you know I'll give the horses their feed before I go down the back, so you can rest a while. I'll come in when I'm done."

"Oh thanks, Allan. You don't need to do that, you know, but I'm sure they'll be happy not having to wait longer. I do hope I'm not causing trouble for you or keeping you from important things. I really appreciate your help today."

"Don't you worry yourself, Mrs. Oaks. I'm always happy to come here; you know that. Hey, who've you got there? Someone new?"

"Take a second and come over here and meet Blue," she replied. "Blue, meet Allan, the young man who comes to help me out some-times. Allan, meet Blue, my little cat come home to stay."

Blue drew as close to the old woman as he could but didn't flinch as Allan gently put out his hand and scratched the back of Blue's neck. He sat very still and looked hard into Allan's clear, blue eyes, sizing him up quickly. He knew in an instant that this wasn't one of those rough, careless men, so he gave Allan's hand a slight rub with his neck.

"Ah, good," said the old woman; "I hoped you two would be friends."

"He's a handsome fella, Mrs. Oaks and he's come at the right time. Well, I'm off. I'll have time to help you turn the horses out when I finish. See you soon!"

As Allan closed the door behind himself, the old woman poured herself another cup of tea and added milk from the pitcher, settling back in her chair. "I can use this extra rest, this morning, fella, but what about you? Do you want to go outside and help Allan? I can see you're as curious as can be. Go on if you want to. I can sit alone for a while."

The little cat stepped back up on the window sill to see what was going on. He looked back and forth from the woman to the man outside. Seeing Allan go to the barn, Blue thought he'd like to go with him, but looking back at the woman again, he decided it was too soon to leave her alone. He'd better stay extra close for a while longer. So he settled down on the sill where he could be close to her but also watch what went on outside.

Before long he saw Allan come out of the barn and go to the old shed where he got a long-handled shovel and a two-wheeled cart. Blue saw him put some large white stones in the cart before pulling it over and gently lifting the burlap-covered form and placing it carefully alongside the stones. Blue liked what he saw; the man was so gentle and caring. Blue settled down a little more, calmly watching the fellow swing the shovel over one shoulder and draw the cart behind him across the yard and down the gentle slope to the big old apple tree. There he set quietly and steadily to his work.

Blue swivelled his head back to the old woman as he heard the legs of her chair scrape against the floor. "Finished my tea, little fella," she said. "It's time to tidy up. Allan or no Allan, we can't stay inside on such a lovely day as this."

Eager to help, Blue hopped from the sill to her empty chair and on down to the floor, taking his position beside her left leg. She gathered the few dishes and took them to the sink, where she started the water running and added soap. A beautiful bubble popped

from the top of the yellow soap bottle and rose slightly before gently drifting downward. Blue was alert in a flash, crouching softly,
watching intently as the shimmery thing approached. Suddenly he
sprang straight up, paws extended, and snatched the bubble from
the air. But what a shock! There was nothing there, at least nothing
but a slippery, wet spot on each paw.

The old woman chuckled as Blue sat down and looked from paw
to paw before licking at them. And what a foul taste! He drew back
slightly then frantically began licking other parts of his paws, trying
to get rid of the soapy taste from his tongue. She laughed again.
"Oh Blue," she said, "you're delightful. Here, I'll wipe your paws
off." He thought the bad taste was almost worth the pleasure she
seemed to have and the gentle care she gave him as she cleaned
him with a soft towel.

"Mind you," she said, "I can't imagine how long it will take me
to get things done if I keep stopping to watch your antics. It has
never taken me this long to wash up a few dishes!" Blue rubbed
against her leg as she washed and dried her things, moving only
when she fetched his saucer and washed it up and then put the milk
pitcher back in the ice box.

"Now," she said, "we'll just fill the wood box by the stove and
then sweep up before we go outside." Again Blue followed her from
the wood box on the verandah to the wood box by the stove, going
back and forth several times. Then she took the corn broom from
its corner in the storage room and began to sweep out the kitchen.
This was fun! Blue dashed back and forth in front of the broom,
slowing progress considerably. He always seemed to be just where
she was sweeping, but she just chuckled and gently pushed him
away. When the kitchen and store room were both swept, she
changed from slippers to shoes and stepped out to sweep off the
verandah. Here a lot more dirt flew ahead of the broom, and Blue
chased bits that she flicked about, catching little wood chips and
playing with them.

As she finished, she saw Allan coming back across the field.
"Time to begin, Blue. You know this hasn't been quite the way

mornings usually begin, don't you? But it's barn time now, little fella. I'd better slip my coat on, though. I feel the chill this morning." As she buttoned her coat, she walked down the steps to meet Allan, the little cat just to her left as if he'd always been there.

CHAPTER NINE

THE BARN CHORES

The old woman quickly brushed one stray tear away as she glanced at the empty spot by the verandah, glad to have both Blue and Allan with her this morning. She turned to Allan as he came up from replacing the tools in the shed. "Okay?" she asked.

"Yes, Ma'am, though I'm awful sorry. I marked the spot with white stones that you like and I planted some daffodil bulbs along the top. Hope that's okay with you. Seemed it would be nicer in spring if I did that." He, too, brushed at a cheek, but quickly turned his attention to the little cat. "I've got something in the van for you, little guy, but first we'd better let those horses out. Ready Mrs. Oaks?"

"Ready," she said, and the three of them headed toward the barn. Inside, Blue quickly ran up the post to the rafters above the horse stalls. He thought he liked the old horses, but he didn't know them well yet and he wasn't going to take chances down there among those big beasts. The old woman chuckled again and said, "You're pretty smart, too, aren't you, scrambling up there where you can boss us about without being trampled? Good puss."

"I guess you don't let them out all higgledy-piggledy, do you, Mrs. Oaks? Can't imagine such chaos at your place."

She smiled gratefully. "You're right, Allan. No sense having a big ruckus when you can have order. These are very quiet horses but only part of that comes from their age. Part is the order and care they have here. Fawn always leads out in the morning. You open the big doors and I'll open her stall when you have them open."

With that, Allan grasped the handle and pulled the left-hand tall door aside. The ease with which it moved surprised him and it opened very quickly. "Whew," he gasped, as he caught his balance and then laughed with her.

"I have to keep the tracks well-oiled," she said, "or I wouldn't be able to move it myself."

"I guess you are kind of slight for such a job," he said, moving the right door with less force. He stood to one side as she opened Fawn's stall door and the old buckskin ambled out. He was surprised to see her pause to gently nudge the old lady and wait for the rub on the nose that she always got in return.

"Way you go, old lady," she said, "have a good feed. Should be apples coming down soon. That's a girl." And Fawn ambled out into the sunshine. "Now Rosy, Misty and Jenny before Sarah," she said, and Allan watched in amazement as each horse in turn paused for its morning greeting before ambling outside. He opened Sarah's stall and she gave him a quick sniff before going over to the old woman for her petting. Allan couldn't help but laugh as the little donkey bent her head down and waited after she'd had her nose rubbed. "Oh, you old mule," said the woman, as she stroked the long ears.

"Silliest thing," she said to Allan, "has to have her ears stroked every morning. Even then she doesn't go out for a while. She'll follow me around a bit before she goes out with the others. You can go ahead. I'll be fine. Thanks for all your help."

"I've never seen them go out before; only been here when you let them in. That's not quite as quiet, is it? You be careful at night now. I do need to go; have a job over at the old McCullough place. Dad sent some cat food out; thought you might need it for your new friend. I'll just get it from the van before I get on my way." Looking up to the rafters, he said, "Are you comin' puss? I've got some food for you."

Blue jumped down to a shelf and then onto the table, but he didn't follow Allan. Instead, he went over the half-door that closed the alley from the feed rooms and doorway and trotted to the old woman, carefully avoiding Sarah's feet. He took up his position next to his friend's left leg and there he remained. She chuckled and said, "Guess he's not ready to go with strangers, not even for food. I'll come and get it." Sure enough, the little cat followed faithfully at her side as she went along with Allan to the van.

"I've never seen such a cat," he said. "He follows you like a dog."

He's sure a fine fellow. Here you go. That should last until next feed day." He passed her the bag of kibbles and climbed into the van. "I won't have to worry about backing over that cat," he said. "So long as I stay away from you, I know he'll be safe!"

"Thanks again, Allan. I don't know what I'd do without your help. You have a good day."

"Call me if you need anything else," he said with a wave as he backed around and then drove down the long drive.

"Well, Blue," she said, "it's just you and me now, and we've chores to do. Let's go see if Sarah is still waiting. She likes to hang around until I've filled the water buckets."

The little cat trotted happily at her side as they returned to the barn. He dropped a little behind, though, as they approached the mule. He wasn't sure about this beast. He decided to tuck himself into the corner and study this a while. The old woman unwound a long hose and quietly moved from stall to stall, filling the bucket in each one. The little mule moved close for a rub each time the woman emerged from one stall to move to the next one, and each time the woman paused and gave a gentle pat or scratch or rub.

The little cat began to feel quite safe. This was not an angry, impatient cow, after all. It was a gentle little mule. He ventured out of his corner and took up his place by the woman's side. Noticing him, Sarah bent her head down to his level and stood perfectly still. They looked at each other a long time, eye to eyes. The old woman watched quietly, waiting, careful not to disturb them. Finally, Blue swung his body around and rubbed against the mule's nose a few times before ambling back to the woman. Sarah raised her head slowly and also walked over, pausing for her last scratch before ambling out into the sunshine.

"Funny, isn't she, Blue? It's the only way she's really different from the horses. She seems to need a little extra cuddling, but she's just fine." Now, help me wind up this hose and get the manure fork. We've some shovelling to do. Blue watched as she went to the large reel above the tap on the wall and turned the handle around and around, drawing the hose up several inches at a time. He was unable to resist the movement and began to chase the hose, batting it with his paws, clasping and pouncing as it dragged along the floor. Once again the woman's chuckle spilled from her as she watched the little cat. She decided to let the nozzle hang down a little so he could continue his play as she went for the cart and fork.

But he still wasn't prepared to leave her, not even for a swinging hose, so he took up his position by her side. "I've had to make quite a few changes in the last few years," she said, as she wheeled the cart up to the first stall. "First I had the long hose put in because the buckets were too heavy for me to carry when they were full. Then I had to get this two-wheeled cart when the wheelbarrow got too hard for me to push. I can pull this, and with its two wheels it moves more easily. Luckily, I already had this special fork. Josiah made this handle when he fixed the axe and the shovel handles for me. This one is a little thinner and shorter than his was, much better for me. I've had to shorten the chores a little, though. I used to lift the horses' bedding each day; now I just clean the soiled parts of four stalls and lift the fifth, doing a different one completely each day. It's still better than most horses get. Besides, I have Allan come in every month to clean the stalls out completely and put fresh bedding in."

The little cat followed her from stall to stall, playing with the few pieces that fell from her fork and running back and forth beneath the cart. He investigated each stall thoroughly and did a little digging himself. It was fun to flick the light peat and shavings mix she used for bedding. He chased the odd bit of rough hay the horses had left, too. When he grew tired of that play, he settled himself in the sunny spot just inside the door and watched the woman on one side and the birds flitting about the oak tree in the centre of the paddock. He rose to follow when the woman began to pull the cart outside. He kept clear of the cart wheels as they crossed over to the large manure pit where she tipped the cart, emptying it deftly. She gave it a little shake to get the last of the dirt out before returning the cart to its place in the barn.

"Before I sweep, we'll have a little break, shall we, Blue? You haven't had your kibbles or your brushing today. Mustn't forget you," she said as she moved toward the shelf where his saucers were. "Remind me to take the new kibbles inside when we go. I can leave a saucer down on your mat there without worrying the mice will come around. That way you can eat whenever you want."

She swept up the barn while the little cat ate, then took his brush and, scooping him into her arms, groomed him carefully. The purr exploded from deep within him as she brushed his coat until all the loose hairs were gone.

"That's a fine fellow," she said. "It's time for lunch and a rest before we do the wood. You going up in the loft?" she asked.

He looked longingly at the place he so loved to sleep before looking back at the old woman. 'No,' he thought, 'not yet. I'll go inside with her.' With that, he hopped down and rubbed against her ankle. Again she chuckled, that rich, satisfied chuckle, as she walked toward the house, the little cat following determinedly by her side.

CHAPTER TEN

NOON NAP

As they entered the house, the little cat wondered what was next. He wasn't used to following anyone else about, having always come and gone as he pleased and been ignored by most everybody. It was much better having someone to look after and was kind of fun waiting to see what would happen next. He kind of hoped there would be a rest before too long; he was used to having many naps during the days and he'd been up a long while this day.

The old woman was having similar thoughts. She, too, was a little tired and she, too, enjoyed wondering what Blue would do next and just how long he would stick so close by her side. He continued following back and forth as she stoked up the fire a little, put the small pot of soup on the hottest part of the stove top so it would heat quickly and set the kettle on to boil. Once again, he followed her from cupboard to table as she put out her few dishes. This time, though, she remembered she'd promised him his own inside dish of kibbles and she paused to rummage in the cupboards a while. "I'm looking for just the right dish," she said, "something for your own. Ah, here it is!"

Blue tipped his head slightly to one side as he looked up at her, sensing that she had something for him and that she was pleased with it. As she moved to another cupboard and reached up again, he tipped his head slightly to the other side and perked his ears up a little straighter, waiting to see what she had. "Here's the old biscuit tin," she said, lifting a tall round tin with pretty pictures painted all around it down to the counter top. "We'll keep your kibbles in here," she said, as she poured all but a few of the kibbles from the bag Allan had brought into the pretty tin. "This will keep them dry and fresh," she said, "and we'll keep it in the pantry." The little cat followed her into the pantry and watched her place it on a shelf just inside the doorway, then followed her back to the counter, where she put the rest of the kibbles into a round, blue dish.

"There," she said, as she bent to put the special dish down on his little mat. "Your very own dish. I won it years ago at the Fall Fair. It's about the right size but is nice and heavy so it won't tip over easily. Like it?"

He rubbed firmly against her arm before rolling right over on the mat in front of the dish. Yes, he was a happy little cat. Though he wasn't really hungry, having eaten in the barn, he sampled a couple of the kibbles just for good measure, then sat quietly by his bowl watching her get her soup and have her small lunch. He could hardly keep himself from lying down for a nap, but he needed to see what she was going to do next, so he sat patiently.

It wasn't long before she pushed her bowl back and patted her lap saying, "Soup is done. Come up while I finish my tea." He sprang up onto her lap and settled down against her tummy, purring rapidly. There they sat until both heads nodded a little. Quickly, she snapped her head up and said, "None of this, little fellow. No napping until the mess is cleaned up." So he hopped down and she cleared the table, washed and wiped the dishes and put them away. Only when the counter and table were wiped and the teapot put back in its spot on the warming shelf did she settle into the rocker. "I don't lie down in the afternoon much, Blue, just take my little nap here by the stove. You sleep where you want."

He couldn't believe his good fortune! Up he hopped and stretched himself full-length on her lap, his little chin stretched out and resting on her arm. With a purr from him and a contented sigh from her, the two drifted quickly to sleep. Already, much of their daily routine was in place. Blue now knew the meal routine, the morning chores, and the wood chopping chores. There would be more to learn, of course, but they'd made a good start. Most important of all, he knew he had a safe place and a person to love. The old rocker rolled slightly back and forth as the two refreshed themselves for what came next.

CHAPTER ELEVEN

EVENING CHORES

That afternoon, Blue helped with the wood as he had done so many times before. As always, they took their little rest when they were halfway through and, as always, they cut and stacked the "extra" piece. When they were finished, there was another meal, the cleaning up and a quiet time together. As they sat at the table, she sipping an extra cup of tea and Blue purring happily on her lap, she chattered a little about what was to come.

"The evening barn chores are nice, Blue, some of my favourite. We'll go out and I'll put the feed in their troughs and the horses will come in. Partly they just know the time and partly they hear me. Every night I groom one horse or the little donkey. That way they each get a good grooming and a careful check over at least once a week. It's a pleasant time, Blue, but I must admit to you that I'm a little anxious tonight. I've never let the horses in without Old Rex to help me. They're real good horses and wouldn't hurt anyone intentionally, but he's always been there to give a little woof or even a nip if anyone gets out of line in her eagerness to get her feed. I always felt safe with him there. There has never been any trouble, for the horses are well-fed and have good pasture, so are not desperate for their feed, but it does seem to be their favourite meal and they are a little livelier than at any other time of day. Well, I'll be sure to stand off to the side and will just pray for the best. When we're done the grooming, we sweep up the barn again before shutting up for the night. Then we have the rest of the evening for knitting. Well, no sense putting it off; I'm sure they will be alright, aren't you?"

He hopped down as she stood up to get her coat and shoes on. He trotted at her side, hoping to chase away the little strain that had come over her. He wondered if he should stay by her side or try sitting at one side of the door as he imagined Rex would have had to do if he was to woof at the horses. He couldn't woof, of course, but maybe they'd respond to a hiss. Oh, but they were big things. Still, he could run fast, so if he was careful he could always try. He began to feel a little anxious too; his hair rose along his back and his eyes grew wide. Still, he trotted by her side as she moved from feed room to the stalls and back again. She tossed a portion of hay into the manger of each stall and then scooped a portion of oats from the tin-lined feed bin at the end of the feed room into each feed trough.

Sure enough, as he trotted back and forth beside her, he could hear the horses moving toward the barn. He glanced up at the old woman several times, hoping to get a hint of how he could best help, but she was intent on filling the last of the feed troughs. The horses were moving more quickly than they had in the morning, but they weren't running; in fact, they were only walking but it sounded loud because they were all together. "Let's just stand to the side here, Blue," she said; "I'm sure they'll just go into their stalls like they always have. I'll just have to tell them to be good."

She stepped to the side, standing in the little protected area just inside the door, and Blue took up his position by her left foot. Steadily and evenly, she began to talk as the horses jostled toward the barn doors. "Just be steady, ladies. There's no need to rush. Nobody will take your food, you know. Steady now. Quiet. One at a time. No crowding in the doorway. That's it; Fawn first. Steady you go, old girl, straight to your stall. That's it. Hush now, Rosy. No dawdling in the alley. Good girl, Misty; move on so Jenny can get in. That's it. Good girls. Well, come on, Sarah, you too." But Sarah stopped in the doorway and lowered her head. "You old mule," said the woman softly as she gave the long ears a rub. "Now get in there and eat."

Sarah ambled into her stall, and the little cat followed the woman as she closed each of the stall doors. "There," she said, a smile returning to her face, "it was just fine, wasn't it, Blue? We'll be okay. They are good horses, aren't they? It's just that they are so much bigger than I am, and people must always be very careful around horses. Easy to get squished in a rush, you know. But we did it. They were good. Tomorrow will be a little easier now that we know we can do it alone. Come on, now, let's carry on. Whose turn is it for grooming tonight? Oh yes, it's Jenny's turn."

Blue sensed that he was free to roam the barn for a while, so while the old woman got the grooming caddy, haltered Old Jenny and tethered her loosely to the ring on the barn wall, he went up the post to the rafters and walked lithely along and across, along and across, watching the horses beneath him. Finding a comfortable spot above Sarah's stall, he sat down to watch. He liked the sounds of this barn. The horses chewed their hay quietly, steadily, rhythmically; it was a soothing sound. Even the occasional snort wasn't alarming at all. The rustling sound as a horse pulled another mouthful of hay from the manger was also a pleasant sound and even with all the horses inside, this barn smelled nice.

Watching the old woman methodically brush Jenny, moving with firm even strokes from her neck down to her hind end, first one side then the other, he felt another rush of the warmth and contentment that had come over him so often since he'd made his choice. He could hear the woman talking to Jenny, fondly calling her 'the old grey mare' and reminding her of how beautiful and special she was. He thought this might be a good time to meet the mare, so he trotted along the rafters to the wall where he could hop to the ledge above the stall, then down to the top of the half-door of the stall and onto the floor. He moved over beside the old woman and gave her a quick rub before sitting next to her and looking up at Jenny.

"So you want to meet Jenny, do you? Stay to her front and you'll be fine," she said, as she moved to trade the curry comb for a fine brush she used for their faces. Blue moved a little closer to Jenny's head and tipped his head slightly to one side as he looked up. Patiently he waited. Finally, she lowered her head just a little and looked at him steadily. She lowered her head further and they looked at each other a while, each silent. Satisfied, the little cat twisted in his own funny way to put the back of his head down on the floor and flop over onto his back. It was almost a somersault, one he did when he was really happy. Seeing him as she came up with the fine brush, the old woman gasped. "Either you're crazy or you have some form of communication I don't understand," she said. "I'd never lie down in front of a horse."

The little cat stayed there, stretching and rolling from side to side, as the woman carefully brushed around Jenny's eyes and ears. "This is Jenny's favorite part, Blue," she said; "watch her push her head into my belly as I brush her nose. If she were a cat, I think she'd purr now." Blue watched as the woman brushed and brushed. He knew how happy Jenny felt. "Can't brush forever, old girl," said the woman as she went back to the grooming caddy. "I'd better pick your hooves."

Jenny reached as far down as the rope would let her and pushed her nose gently against Blue's tummy. He flopped to the other side and she nudged him gently again. Then he flipped into a sitting position, gave her a steady glance and trotted over to the woman's side. Jenny lifted her head as the woman moved to her right front foot. "Good girl," she said, and Jenny bent her knee, lifting her hoof to be picked. The woman flicked the bit of packed dirt out of the crevices on the hoof and gave it a quick brush. "Looks pretty good, Jen," she said, "no chips or cracks. Good girl."

The little cat watched in amazement as the woman moved from hoof to hoof, cleaning and brushing. He wasn't sure if he'd like to have his feet picked like that, but it didn't seem to bother Jenny. The old horse stood very quietly, making the job much easier than it might have been if the woman had had to lift and hold instead of just rest the hoof in one hand as she picked with the other.

When she was finished the hooves, the woman took another brush and cleaned and tidied Jenny's tail and mane. "There you are, old girl; just lovely now. You could still win ribbons in a parade, you know. You're a real beauty." Jenny bobbed her head up and down a little as if to agree. Blue hopped up onto a ledge as the woman untied the rope and led Jenny back to her stall. She hung the halter neatly on its hook, replaced the grooming tools on their shelf and deftly swept up the bit of mess.

"What do you, think, Blue? Shall we give them a treat for being so good coming in tonight? There's a sack of carrots in the feed room. We'll chop some up for them." Blue trotted by her side then leapt up onto the table to watch her chop carrots into a bucket. Then he followed her along the alley as she dumped a few pieces into each feed trough. Soon the barn was filled with a new kind of sound, a deep crunch-crunch echoing in the huge mouths followed by the lowest munching sound he'd ever heard. It sounded good to him.

Carefully the woman closed the big barn doors and returned to the feed room. "That's it for tonight, Blue. Let's go."

"Good night, horses. Good night, little mule," she called as they stepped out into the gathering dusk, closed the bottom and top of the narrower barn door and headed toward the house.

"It's still quite light, Blue, but before long we'll be doing these chores by lantern, even if we start earlier. The evenings will be long soon. But that will be just fine now that you are here to sit with me. We'll have a comfy fall and winter, won't we?" she asked. In response, the little cat ran ahead of her on the path, leapt up the steps and, turning to face her, sat down and waited as if to say, "yes we will."

Chapter Twelve

A Night Inside

The evening was not too chilly, so the old woman didn't light the fire in the fireplace before settling down to knit. The little cat followed her about as she made herself a cup of tea and got all her things ready near the rocker by the fireplace. She took the worn book from the coffee table and put it on a footstool in front of the chair. She lit two lanterns, one on the table by her chair and the other on the mantle, so she would have plenty of light as it grew darker. Then she put teapot, cup and saucer, spoon and little pitcher of cream on a tea trolley and pushed that up near the chair as well.

Blue began to wonder if they'd ever be finished going back and forth. He hoped they'd stop soon, for he had spied a wonderful looking place for him to curl up. The tea trolley had an empty shelf beneath the tray that the tea sat on. He'd be very safe on a low shelf between the large wooden wheels that would partially obscure people's view of him, and the shelf looked invitingly smooth. Of course, he'd also noted the footstool with its tapestry top, but the woman had covered that with the book. The window sills weren't inviting in the twilight. Somehow he didn't think he could always sit on her lap.

Finally, everything was ready and the woman sank down into her rocker. "This is another good time of day, little fella," she said. "I never tire of the old stories and truth in the Good Book; they warm me almost as much as the fire does in the winter nights. And it's good to have the company while I knit. I enjoy knitting tremendously; it's one of the few ways I still have of doing for people. I promised you a little blanket of your own, so I'll get on with that tonight. Then I'll make some good winter gloves for Allan. He won't take any money for the extra things he does for me, but he does like the winter woollens that I knit. Most of the time, though, I make little stuffed animals and small things for children who don't have much. Every once in a while, I do larger things — bedspreads, blankets, shawls and such — to sell. That's the way I get the extra money to get more wool when I run out. You won't want to be up on my knee with these needles flying, though, so you'll have to find a comfy place of your own."

The little cat walked around the woman's chair and tables as she poured her tea, lifted the book onto her lap and found the page she wanted, picked up needles and wool and began her evening's pleasure. He rubbed against her legs a few times, wondering whether to choose the stool now that it was empty or the tea trolley. As he looked from one to the other, the woman lifted one foot and rested it on the stool, giving a slight sigh of relief as she did so.

"That feels better," she said, and she rocked slowly, needles moving rapidly, eyes on the book on her lap. The little cat knew, then, the place for him. After a couple more rubs against her ankle and a glance up at her, he moved to the tea trolley, stepped carefully onto the shelf and sat down. He quickly washed his front paws, his ears and his face before curling himself into a comfortable ball and tucking his tail around him. With the rhythmic, soothing sound of knitting needles clicking in his ears, he dozed into a delicious sleep.

'I guess there's no sense reading aloud tonight,' the woman thought. 'The little fella is pretty tired after his first day, too tired even to play with the wool. It will get easier for him here, once he settles in. I'm sure glad he came to stay.'

Much later, the little cat heard the woman putting her needles into the basket. "There," she said, "I've done a little blanket for you. Guess you want it here on the tea trolley, do you?" She reached down and put a soft, thick, blue blanket beside him. He stretched and yawned, a wide, wide yawn, before reaching his paw out and tugging a little at the blanket. He looked as if he were patting it as he investigated it with his little mostly-white paws. Then he put his head down on the blanket and rubbed back and forth. It was soft and it was pretty, but best of all, it smelled just like her! The purr exploded from his chest.

"That's it for tonight, Blue;" she said, "we've to get a good sleep so we stay healthy. Let's tidy up and bank the fire before we get ready for bed." He stretched again while she blew out one lantern and placed the other on the tea trolley. Then he followed her as she pushed the trolley into the kitchen. The light of the lantern made odd shadows that changed shape as it moved along. Blue, used to complete darkness at night, stayed close to his friend's leg. He wondered what "get ready for bed" meant but he knew he'd find out if he stuck close to the old woman.

After she tidied up her tea things, poked about in the old stove and adjusted some little knobs on its side and on the stove pipe, she took the lantern in one hand and patted her thigh with the other. "C'mon, little fella; you can sleep with me," she said as she went into the bedroom.

Blue watched her put the lantern on the little table by the bed and then get into her night things. He sat looking at the inviting big bed, wondering what it would feel like. It looked somehow softer than the big bales and piles of hay he usually found to sleep in, but he didn't know if he should hop up there or not so he sat patiently on the little mat beside the bed. He didn't have to wonder very long. The old woman turned back the covers from two fluffy pillows and got into one side of the bed, pulling the covers up over her as she leaned back on one pillow. "Coming up?" she asked, patting the bed beside her, and the little cat crouched and sprang lightly onto the bed.

Never had he walked on such a beautiful thing. His little feet left tiny indents in the fluffy lazy daisy quilt as he tiptoed along the bed. Nothing scratched or poked at him anywhere. He walked about the bed for a while, investigating every inch. Stepping onto the pillow, he was surprised at how far down his foot sank and he pulled it back, returning to the firmer quilt. The woman chuckled at his surprise, and he suddenly had that warm feeling again. He tried the pillow again, braver this time, and was pleased to find it hollow into his shape. He'd chosen his spot. As the woman turned down the lamp and blew it out, the little cat settled into the pillow right close to her and began to purr. The old woman drifted dreamily to sleep, lulled by the gentle purrs rising from her little friend.

Blue slept on and off most of his first night indoors. Never had it been so quiet, so dry, so warm in all his life. Never had he felt so safe. As often as he drifted happily to sleep, he'd waken to listen for a while to the gentle breathing beside him and to enjoy the warmth and the dryness. Several times he hopped down from the warm bed and padded almost silently through the house as if checking that all was well. Always he returned to curl up in the nest of his pillow and sleep a while longer. Several times in the night, the little purr rumbled from deep within his chest as he felt the slight rising and falling of the covers or felt the warm breath of the woman sleeping next to him. For the first time ever, Blue purred in his sleep.

CHAPTER THIRTEEN

PASTURES AND A PROBLEM

In the days that followed, the little cat never regretted his choice. He and the old woman moved happily about the old farm, tending to the horses and little donkey, looking after the wood, cooking pots of soup and stew, baking bread, gathering the ripening apples and preserving them and doing the same with the fall vegetables. He enjoyed pulling the carrots from the patch and storing them in layers of sand, some for the horses and some for the woman. It was great fun, scrambling after the dirt balls that fell from the carrots when the woman shook them and even more fun batting the bushy carrot tops while she cut them from the carrots. In the evenings, he played with her wool, batting the balls across the floor and pouncing on the moving twine. Other times, he slept on his little blanket while her knitting needles clicked away. Always he slept on the pillow beside her at night.

As he came to see she knew he was staying and that she was happy, he sometimes left her side to do some investigating of his own, chasing the odd spider in the barn, chasing leaves in the orchard as they tumbled to the ground, even chasing the odd field mouse that dared come by. But he never stayed away long, nor did he go very far from her side.

One morning she said they'd have to go down to the pasture before they turned the horses out, and he trotted happily at her side as they walked farther down the back than they'd gone before. "It's time to close the gate to the south pasture and open the gate to the north one," she said as they walked along. "I kept them out of the north one until we got the apples we needed. Now I'll let them in so they can pick up the windfalls and nibble the nice apples left higher than I could reach. See how those apple trees hang over the fence between the orchard and the pasture, Blue? The horses like that. Have to rotate the pastures anyway so I plan the rotation around the apple season." She closed the gate to the south pasture

51

and opened the one to the north. Blue scampered between the rails and into the north pasture, unable to resist the unnibbled grass.

The old woman stood and laughed as he leapt about, springing onto things she couldn't see. Over and over again, he'd crouch down then suddenly pounce several feet ahead of where he'd been. He looked like a wild kitten, chasing after anything that moved and even things that didn't. What fun!

"Oh, Blue," she said, "I think you're imagining things, leaping all about like that. What a funny puss you are. But I can't stand and watch all day. I have to go back and let the horses out. They'll be almost as happy as you are when they amble down here and see they have both the lusher pasture and the fallen apples."

Blue chose to return with her, once again trotting happily at her side, meowing occasionally. His friend seemed strangely quiet after her nice laughing time in the pasture, and Blue lost the warm feeling he had so much since he'd come home. His usually erect little ears turned part way out and down a little as he pondered this strange feeling, and he meowed more loudly and a little questioningly. The woman seemed not to notice his concern as she continued up the gentle slope toward the barn. He meowed more loudly and inched closer to her leg, careful not to trip her but trying to close this sudden distance between them. Still, she carried on, intent on the barn it seemed. Blue continued his meowing, using the short, scolding meows he'd almost forgotten. She walked on. When they reached the barn, the little cat saw his chance. As she paused to open the half-door, he scurried in front of her and rubbed against her legs, scolding loudly.

She seemed to snap out of her reverie. "I'm sorry, little puss. I wasn't good company, was I? Don't scold me so. I am sorry. Come, we'll sit a minute before turning the horses out," she said, as she moved toward a stool near the barn door. Sitting down, she took the little cat onto her lap and stroked his back. He could feel some tiredness in her, so he rubbed the side of his face against her chin and meowed softly, gently.

"Oh, Blue," she said. "It's just that winter is coming and everything is so much harder in the winter. Down there in the pasture, watching you frolic about, I remembered the two times I could have trouble with the horses. Even the old girls get a little frolicsome in the early spring, and there's no Rex to keep them in line. What's worse, though, is that they are quite wild in the first snowfall, especially Rosy. I don't know what it is, maybe the brightness of it, but she gets quite giddy and runs, bucks and rolls like a filly when I let her out. The others aren't quite as bad, but they, too, do a lot of running and leaping around in the snow. Oh, they're not mean, just excited, but what will I do without Rex? I just don't know what to do. I can't get a puppy; puppies are too energetic and eager for old people like me and not much use for old horses either. I can't stand the thought of getting rid of the horses, not for them or for me. Well, we've managed so far, you and I. We'll just have to pray and to expect we'll continue to manage. At any rate, it will be a while before the first snowfall yet, so we may as well continue to enjoy our life. No sense borrowing trouble."

The little cat reached one paw out and laid it gently on the woman's free hand while arching his back up into the hand that continued to stroke him. He must make the happiness return to her, must chase this care away. He could see there was a problem, one he'd have to think about, but first he had to help his friend. He began to rub gently back and forth against her tummy, purring softly as he moved. Each time he turned on her knee to rub against her with his other side, his tail flicked across the softly wrinkled cheek, tickling her slightly. He continued his purring, turning and flicking until finally the crease in her forehead relaxed and a smile tugged at the corners of her mouth.

"Oh, Blue," she said, "you're tickling me with your old tail. Fine puss you are, tickling a tired old woman! What a clown, a real good clown, aren't you? Let's get on with it, then. The horses are waiting." With a quick little hug before putting him on the ground, the woman got up, refreshed, and went into the barn to face the day, her little cat trotting lightly at her side. He may not be a dog who could bark and boss horses about, but he knew that somehow he helped when he stayed by her side.

CHAPTER FOURTEEN

BLUE IS PUZZLED

That day when they began the wood-chopping chores, Blue was surprised to see the number of rounds the woman took down to be chopped. The pile looked huge to him, but he took up his spot on the block in the doorway as usual. As he followed the swing of the axe with his head, his thoughts returned to the problem he'd learned in the morning and he wondered what he, a little cat, could do about it. He'd made friends with all the horses as well as the little donkey. He wasn't surprised that Rosy would be the problem. She was the only one who sometimes was a little careless of him. The others stood very still when he walked beneath them. Jenny even let him play with her tail, and the little mule let him curl up next to her when she was lying down. Rosy was never mean, but she sometimes just forgot everything around her, so set she was on something in her own mind. Sometimes it was just going in or out that made her forget everything else; sometimes it was her food. Other times it was her preoccupation with the wind that made her forget everything else. He had learned to be careful around her. That wasn't much help, was it?

His little face took on a puzzled look as the sound of chopping stopped. There was much more than half the pile left, but the woman was coming for her rest. He moved aside, and she sat on the stump, taking him onto her lap.

"We get two short rests today, Blue. It's chilly in the evenings now, so I'll be lighting the fireplace. That means we have to cut more wood, so I take two rests instead of one. Did you wonder if I'd lost count? No, it's just the weather changing. When the snow comes, we'll not only have to cut even more wood, but it takes longer to take it to the house because it's slippery under foot. It's good, healthy work, though, and I wouldn't trade my old stove and fireplace for anything. We can manage the wood just fine, can't we? I like the fresh air, too, don't you?" The little cat purred louder and

55

pushed more closely into her tummy.

When she resumed her work, he continued puzzling over the problem. 'Or do we have two problems?' he wondered as he watched the axe rise and fall. 'First, the horses are going to get frisky and that makes her nervous without old Rex here to help her out, and now I find there's much more chopping to do and it takes longer to get the wood into the house. What can a little cat do about these things?'

Blue thought and thought. There must be something he could do, but he couldn't figure it out. Even the extra chopping time wasn't enough for him to puzzle out any solution to the problem. He was stumped.

He decided to take part of his afternoon nap in the barn, thinking he might come up with a solution out there. He nestled into his little hollow of hay and had a quick cat-nap but couldn't sleep long. Soon, he was up wandering along the rafters, pacing about, looking for a solution. He leapt down and walked back and forth in front of the large doors, wondering how he could boss those horses about like Rex had. Back and forth he went, pacing and pacing. Finally he sat down to one side of the doors, staring at the doorway, picturing the horses coming in at night, first Fawn then Rosy, Misty, Jenny and Sarah. They always came in the same order. Surely they would also always be calm, wouldn't they? He guessed not or the woman wouldn't be worried. He stared and thought and thought and stared. What a puzzle! But he'd better go into the house before the woman worried about him. At least he could save her that trouble.

He meowed softly at the back door and she let him in with a smile. "Have a good sleep?" she asked, and he rubbed up against her ankle and purred, glad to see her cheerful. Maybe it wasn't such a problem after all. Despite the warmth of the woman and the house, though, Blue couldn't fully chase the problem from his mind. It seemed there to pester him for good. He'd have to try something.

That night when they went out to let the horses in, Blue had an idea. He'd see just what he could do. When the old woman went to stand in the little hollow by the door and talk soothingly to the horses, Blue sat just outside the door and off to the side, crouched slightly instead of sitting erect as he usually did. Fawn came in steadily as usual and even Rosy walked straight to her stall. As she often did, though, Misty paused in the doorway, blocking the way. Here was his chance. The little cat arched his back and hissed with all his might. Misty just swung her head around and looked at him as if to say, "what's the silly fuss about?" before sauntering into her stall.

Blue heard the old woman chuckle quietly. He'd failed with the horses but not, it seemed, with her. When the horses were all in their stalls and their doors were shut, she paused to scoop him into her arms.

"You dear puss," she said, rubbing her cheek against his head. "What you trying to do? Get those old horses moving? That's a mighty good hiss you've got there, but I don't think Misty understood, do you? Never mind, fella. They came in just fine, didn't they? Don't worry. We're a good team, you and I." A small purr rose up into the little cat's throat as he nestled against her neck, but when she put him down to carry on with the chores, the warmth left him again. He had to find a solution to this problem!

The next few days and nights were hard ones for the little cat. He couldn't settle down properly, so puzzled he was. He kept up all his routines and stayed close to the old woman, helping her in the ways he could, but always during the quiet times, the puzzle returned and he grew restless, trying to solve it. No matter how much he thought, he couldn't come up with a way he could help. Over and over he pictured the horses coming in, jostling each other in their eagerness, and over and over, he saw only Old Rex as he imagined him in the doorway, quickly controlling them with a woof and a nip. He couldn't even sleep well, so occupied was he with the puzzle. He found himself pacing around the house at night more than he slept curled up on the pillow.

Finally, after several restless days and nights, he paced the house for the twentieth time one night. Always he imagined Old Rex sitting in the barn doorway. But Old Rex was gone, and Blue was tired. He'd tried and tried and he'd hardly slept for days. He had to go back to bed and sleep a while. In the wee hours of the morning, he hopped softly onto the bed and curled up on his pillow, letting himself listen to the even, warm breathing of his friend. At last he drifted off to sleep, soothed by her nearness and warmth. As he slept, he saw Old Rex sitting in the barn doorway, making everything safe. The little cat stirred in his sleep, troubled even in his dreams. Funny that he had become more worried than the old woman. How could one little cat look after a woman and the horses? He stirred again, restless, puzzled, struggling as he slept.

Through the mists of his dream, a brightness began to spread, moving toward the eye of the little cat. It spread from a distance outward, washing toward him as waves approach the ocean beaches. In a sudden, bright explosion, the little cat was engulfed by the wave. Immediately awake and alert, he sat up on the bed, bumping the woman in his haste. He knew! He knew the answer. He knew what to do. He purred excitedly as the woman stirred beside him. He hoped it was morning so he could do what had to be done to solve the problem.

CHAPTER FIFTEEN

BLUE SETS OUT

"It is time to get up, isn't it, little fella?" said the old woman as she sat up in bed. Blue rubbed against her side before hopping down onto the floor. He trotted into the kitchen, not even waiting for her to dress and make the bed. He had business to attend to. He jumped up onto the chair and stepped onto the window sill where he sat down to look outside. 'The weather will be okay today,' he thought, 'but how will I accomplish this task?' He stared outside, eyes squinted together, planning what he must do. 'I'll wait until after we turn the horses out,' he thought, 'and then go while she's cleaning the barn. That shouldn't worry her too much, but I sure wish there were some other way to do this. I hate to leave her alone. There isn't any choice, though; I have to go and do it. I must solve the problem. I'll just be as quick as I can. I sure hope there's no trouble.'

Having made his plan, the little cat turned his attention to the woman as she came into the kitchen and began stoking the fire, starting her oatmeal and the kettle before going out to feed the horses. Blue stuck extra close to her side, trying to give her all the love and attention he could so she'd know he was good and loyal. He followed her from stall to stall, waiting patiently by her side as she greeted each horse with a rub on the nose and rubbing the donkey's ears as always. Never once did he leave her, not even to check around the barn as he usually did in the morning to make sure no mice had come in to escape the cold nights. He didn't even do any investigating on the way back to the house; he stayed right by her side the whole time.

When she'd finished her oatmeal, he leapt quickly onto her knee and settled down to spend as much time with her as he could. He was glad and a little relieved when she poured a second cup of tea. That would give them some extra time. Besides, as the time grew nearer, he was getting a little nervous. What if things didn't work out? Or what if he were wrong? He really dreaded leaving and did

not look forward to his journey. As he sat on her lap, he wished he
didn't have to go, but when she scratched his ears just the way he
liked it so much, he burst out purring and knew he had to do this
for her.

All too soon, she finished her tea, cleaned up her dishes and got
her barn clothes on. Blue stayed close to her side the whole time,
though he held back just a little as they headed toward the barn.
This would be hard, but he must push himself to do it. He trotted
faster, keeping right beside the woman. He even stayed with her as
she entered the alleyway to let the horses out, not leaving her side.
The horses plodded out, each pausing for her little nudge and pat.
The little cat grew anxious as each one left for the pasture, knowing
his time was drawing nearer. He was relieved that Sarah stuck to
her routine and stayed behind, determined to spend her extra time
with the old woman. Now was his chance to get away without the
woman noticing. He couldn't resist giving a rub up against her leg
just before he turned to go.

While the old woman talked to Sarah and rubbed her long ears,
the little cat left the barn and trotted across the paddock to the edge
of the forest. In the brush beside the tall trees, he paused to look
back, longing to return to the woman. Uncertain, he sat down,
looking into the forest then back at the barn. Oh, how he hated to
go. He never wanted to go back into the forest. He never wanted
to go back across the pasture to the old, dark barn. He never wanted to smell those old cows, hear those harsh men or have to run
from that mean dog again. A little shiver escaped him, and he
crouched down by the tree, looking longingly at the bright barn.
'There must be some other way,' he thought, as he crouched even
closer to the ground, hating the darkness and dampness of the forest. But he knew there wasn't. As he caught the sound of the
woman's voice talking to the little donkey, he knew he had to do it
and he resolved to go bravely onward.

Determinedly, he rose from his crouch and, with a quick glance
back at the barn, turned and headed into the woods. He set an even
trot, his tail up, his ears perked and alert to all sounds around him.

He set his face toward his goal, head slightly down, legs slightly bent, keeping him close to the ground even at a trot. He decided not to stop until he reached his goal, not even at the edge of the forest. As he emerged from the forest, he almost faltered at the sight of the familiar old fields, but he pushed himself onward, not breaking his pace, not daring to pause for reflection or even to check for the men and dog. He'd just trot on past if the men were around and he'd break into a run if he heard the dog. He had outrun him often enough to know he could do it.

So the little cat trotted on, not looking to the left or the right, but heading for the barn. All of a sudden, he heard the low growl just in time to break into a run. Ears flat, he ran and bounded across the field, heart racing, dog right at his tail. Into the barn and up the old post he leapt as the dog snatched the end of his tail between sharp, ugly teeth. The little cat dug his claws in and tugged, letting out a cry of pain as his tail came free. Quickly he scaled the post and crawled out on the rafter, out of reach of the mean dog. Eyes wide, the little cat peered down at the dog standing with his front paws up on the post, a tuft of dark fur sticking from the side of his mouth. The dog's eyes gleamed and the little cat rose, arched his back and spit, his own teeth bared. With a sharp bark, the dog dropped down and walked out of the barn.

The little cat's heart pounded as he sat down on the rafter, eyes fixed on the door, ears alert. He slumped down a little, tired, frightened and sore. Oh, how he hated that dog and this place. The smell seemed worse than it had ever been, and it was damp, dull and dirty. Still, he was safe up on the rafter, so he sat still, trying to rest and calm himself.

Gingerly, he curled his tail around him and licked the end of it. There was a huge chunk of fur missing, almost the whole black tip of the tail, and it was bent and sore just below the raw spot where the fur had ripped out. The little cat licked and licked, trying to ease the hurt and to get the smell of dog off him. After a while, he could smell his own blood and not the dog's mouth any more, but he continued licking, trying to stop the bit of bleeding and hoping the pain would stop. He felt tired all over and very, very cold. He licked more slowly and began looking around for a more comfortable spot where he could recover a bit.

Chapter Sixteen

Blue Finds The Solution

Carefully, he crept along the rafter to the hay loft and stepped into the pile of hay. At the smell of the damp and musty hay, he was reminded of the other barn with its sweet, fresh, dry hay and he shook himself. He had a mission, here, and he must complete it. Giving his tail a few more licks with his tongue, he rose, trotted to the back of the hay loft and looked out through the hole left by one of the broken boards. Not seeing what he wanted, he drew his head back in and trotted to the other side of the loft, poking his head out the square opening and looking way down at the ground below him. There she was!

Quickly he scrambled down the nearest post, pausing to look for the mean dog before jumping to the floor and running out the back of the barn. He began to meow as he rounded the corner and headed toward the broken hay wagon beside the barn. The black dog looked out from under the wagon where she had been sleeping and wagged her tail, letting out a gentle woof as she saw her old friend coming toward her. She pulled herself from beneath the wagon and stretched each of her back legs before eagerly turning to the little cat who now sat, waiting and meowing.

'This is it! She is the solution,' thought the little cat. 'I know it. Now if only I can tell her what I know.'

Meowing continuously, the little cat sat in front of the shaggy dog and stared deep into her eyes, thinking hard about the bright, clean barn, the empty spot by the door, the horses coming in and the gentle, old woman standing carefully to the side. He thought hard about the empty spot between the path and the verandah and the empty winter spot on the verandah by the back door. He thought hard about the woman and the wood. The black dog wagged her tail and gave a few gentle woofs, nudging the little cat with her nose.

'No,' he thought, 'she's not understanding.' So, he stared harder.

He thought about all the hard things the men had said about this dog, that she was useless, that they may as well just shoot her for all the good she was. He thought about her hard life, having to hunt for her own food, having to hide from the rough men, having to scrap with all the cats for drops of spilt milk. He thought about the cold, wet barn and the smelly corners she could hide in.

Then he imagined himself trotting back to the nice farm, the black dog at his heels. He thought about the good woman, reaching down to pat the dog; he thought about good food, warm shelter. Again he imagined the black dog standing by the barn door, woofing at the horses as they entered the barn. And all the while, he meowed and meowed and stared deeply into the dog's eyes, willing her to know that she was the solution to the problem.

Finally, the little cat stood up and rubbed against the dog's shoulder, willing her to follow him. 'Please,' he thought, 'you've got to come. We need you.' With that, he took a few steps away from the dog, meowing pleadingly. The dog cocked her head to one side and crinkled her head just above her floppy ears. She wagged her tail a little.

'Come on,' thought the little cat; 'we need you.' He took a few more steps. This time he decided he'd better keep going while he looked over his shoulder and watched the dog. Sure enough, she got to her feet and began to follow, her head still tipped a little to one side. 'She understands,' thought Blue. 'She knows I need her to follow me,' he thought, as he trotted along beside the barn. After he rounded the corner, staying close to the back of the barn, he slowed down and watched behind to see if she would continue following and was relieved to see her step a little gingerly around the corner and come up behind him.

Carefully they darted past the open back doorway, the dog hesitantly following close behind the little cat, and trotted to the far corner of the barn. There the little cat paused, sitting down close to the barn, the dog sitting just behind him. Cautiously, the cat peered around the corner. Quickly he drew his head back and crouched to the ground. The men and the mean dog were in the field! Blue backed up a few steps, pushing against the dog and crouching close to the ground. They'd have to wait. As the dog lay down behind the cat, her head stretched along the ground beside him, the little cat shivered, afraid the old woman would be missing him by now, afraid he was causing her worry and sadness. But there was nothing he could do. He and the dog would just have to wait until the men left.

CHAPTER SEVENTEEN

BLUE BRINGS THE SOLUTION HOME

Despite Blue's troubled heart, it felt kind of good to lie with the friendly dog again. He snuggled in close, feeling a little safer tucked between the dog and the barn than he would have felt alone. The men never came back here, but he worried about the mean dog. His tail throbbed, and he returned to licking it while they waited. The black dog curled herself around him, trying to shelter him with her thin but long body, nudging him occasionally as he continued his licking. The more his tail hurt, the more Blue longed to get home, and the longer they had to wait, the more worried he became about the old woman. Still, he could hear the men cursing as they worked in the field beyond the barn. The waiting was terrible, but he knew what they could do.

They would be able to leave when the men let the cows in and began their milking. They always commanded the mean dog to stay once they had the cows inside, and Blue knew the dog wouldn't budge an inch once they'd given that command. 'Strange thing,' he thought. 'Those men like the mean, stupid dog who does whatever they yell at him no matter how silly or even indecent it may be, but they don't like the black dog who is gentle and kind and smart enough to do what needs to be done.' He didn't understand that some people value only hunting and watch dogs, not loyal companions, but he did know that it would be safe to leave when the milking began.

Relieved to have a plan, he tried to settle down and wait. The black dog slept a while, but the little cat was too restless to settle that much, too eager to return home. As the shadows grew longer he began to wonder if those old cows would ever come in. He noticed that clouds were rolling in along with the gathering dusk and he tried to get a little closer to the dog as they waited. He felt very cold, huddled there beside the old barn.

Just as the first drops of rain began to fall, the little cat heard the sounds of the men opening the gate and herding the cows into the barn. He sat up tall and nudged the dog awake, but he didn't dare look around the corner. Ears perked up, he listened intently. Wondering what was up, the dog also sat erect, straining her ears, hearing the shoving and bawling of the cows and the cursing of the men. Finally, they heard the man bellow, "Stay!" followed by the sounds of the milk stools scraping and the milk squirting into the dirty tin milk pails.

Quickly, the little cat stepped ahead and peered around the corner of the barn. Sure enough, the mean dog was sitting in front of the open barn door, staring inside the barn at the men milking the cows. Here was their chance. The little cat turned to the dog and looked into her eyes, conveying the need for haste. The dog stood up, ready to follow.

Quickly but quietly the little mostly grey tabby cat, followed closely by the black dog, ran out of the shelter of the barn and into the open field. Not stopping to look to either side, the cat headed straight for the forest, staying as close to the ground as he could while still moving quickly. The dog, sensing his urgency, stayed just behind him, tail down, head close to the ground, large paws moving surprisingly softly through the field. Steadily they made their way across the open field, never slowing down, never swerving. Only when they were past the first few trees at the edge of the forest and into the underbrush did the little cat slow down and dare to rest. He stopped beside a huge tree trunk and carefully shook each paw, hating the wetness he'd had to endure to cross the pasture. The big dog stopped beside him and shook the water from her thick coat, sending a spray in all directions and forcing the little cat to shake as well.

The little cat took a few swipes at his face, trying to get the worst of the water and mud from it, as he peered into the forest, dreading having to cross it in the darkness and having to get even wetter as he moved through the underbrush. The dog stood with her head cocked to one side, her sides heaving slightly from the long run; she hadn't eaten for a long time and wasn't in shape for covering distances quickly. She looked quizzically at the little cat, wondering where he was taking her and what they were doing in the forest. It was so very dark and damp in here, it didn't seem like a better place to be. At least the old barn had a roof over it. The little cat looked back at her, tiredness in his eyes. He wasn't sure he could carry on yet. He was so cold, wet, sore and tired. He wished he'd been able to sleep earlier. He leaned a little against the dog, trying to gather strength.

Suddenly, he sat up straight, his ears perked up, his head turned into the dark forest. Startled by the sudden movement, the dog stood up, her hair ruffled along her back and neck. Still the cat sat unmoving, every part of him strained toward the darkness of the forest, sure he could hear something. Yes! It was the voice of the old woman calling over and over in the night.

Like a streak, he was off, running through the brush, leaping over fallen logs, sending water flying in all directions from the leaves of the underbrush. Tentatively, the dog followed him at a trot, unsure, a little afraid. She slowed to a walk and then stopped as she saw the little cat bolt from the edge of the forest and up onto a paddock fence where a little old woman stood with tears streaming down her face.

"Oh, Blue," she said, "I've been so worried. I thought something had happened to you. I've been out here calling and calling, trying to find you. I knew you wouldn't leave me after you'd come home to stay. I just knew it. Oh, little puss, it's so good to have you back." Ignoring the water and mud that covered the little cat, she scooped him into her arms and rubbed her face against his little wet ear. Overcome, the little cat let out a long double purr, ending with several happy meows. He even reached up and licked the salty cheek.

"Look at you, little fellow," said the old woman, as she turned to go toward the barn, "we'll have to give you a good rub. What on earth compelled you to go out and to be away so long?"

The little cat squirmed in her arms, suddenly remembering his mission. He meowed as he strained away from her body, needing to get down and finish what he'd undertaken. Surprised, the old woman stopped and bent to put the cat down, saying, "What is it? You want to walk?"

Quickly the little cat ran back to the edge of the forest, meowing sharply as he approached the dog. The woman returned to the fence and watched the little cat, straining to see in the darkness. She could see the little fellow sit down, looking toward the dark shadows in the forest. He didn't move a muscle as he meowed repeatedly, demandingly. "What is it, Blue?" she called across the fence, "what do you want?"

The little cat looked deeply into the eyes of the black dog before getting up and rubbing against her front legs. Turning, he walked slowly but determinedly toward the woman. After hesitating a moment, the shaggy, black dog rose and followed slowly behind him, her ebony coat hiding her in the darkness. Reaching the woman, the little cat rubbed back and forth against her legs before sitting down at her side, looking up expectantly at her, meowing his desire that she accept his gift.

As the wet and weary dog ducked under the bottom fence rail to move next to the cat, the woman suddenly saw her through the darkness. She stared in amazement as the muddy, black mound sat down beside the little cat, cocking her head to one side and looking up at the old woman. The little cat moved closer to the dog, meowed softly and leaned against her. He was tired, wet, dirty and sore, but he'd found the solution and brought it home at last.

CHAPTER EIGHTEEN

CLEANED UP

"Mercy, Blue, what is this?" his gentle friend said as she bent and put her hand on the dog's head. "Someone else needs a home?" Blue rose and rubbed against the woman's legs, moving back and forth and purring loudly. She reached farther down and gave one ear a scratch before cupping the dog's chin with one hand and rubbing her head with the other.

"Poor pooch," she said, "you're a mess, all wet, muddy and matted; I'll bet you're hungry, too; I can feel your ribs sticking out even through this matted coat. Doesn't anyone feed you? Come on, then; we'll have to do something for you. Can't leave you out here on a night like this. Besides, I've got to clean little Blue up. Let's go into the barn," she said, scooping Blue up in one arm and heading toward the barn, the dog at her heels.

Inside the barn, one lantern was already lit and hanging in its safe place on the wall. She put Blue down on the table, and the dog moved nearby, sitting as close to the little cat as possible, watching the woman move softly about. She took another lamp from its shelf and lit it, hanging it on another wall where it would light up her work area.

"What will I need?" she wondered aloud as she turned toward the two animals. She couldn't keep a little gasp from escaping as she saw them in the light. "Wait there," she said, as she walked quickly into the feed room and gathered a huge armful of sweet hay.

The dog and cat sat perfectly still, relieved to be inside and safe, wondering a little what she would do. When she returned, she dropped to her knees on the floor in front of the dog, immediately beginning to rub her all over with the dry hay. Gently but briskly she rubbed and rubbed, moving from her head down her back, throwing aside soiled hay and using the clean dry stuff to rub the rest of the dog. In spite of some hesitation, the dog's tail soon began to wag a little, making soft thumping noises on the barn floor. "That a girl," soothed the old woman, "we'll soon have you a little drier and warmer. Then we'll fix Blue up too."

Comforted, the dog willingly lay down and rolled over, letting the woman tackle the muddy, matted fur on her belly. "I can take the worst of it off," said the old woman, "but we'll have to give you a good bath tomorrow. It's too cold, tonight, so we'll have to wait. This is better, though, isn't it? Must feel terrible, all that mud clinging to you. Poor girl." The dog's tail wagged back and forth even as she lay there on her back. She'd never felt quite so good before. Throwing the rest of the soiled hay aside, the woman gave the dog a few rubs with her soft hand before turning to Blue.

"Come on, little fella," she said as she took a towel off the shelf and sat down on the stump below the lantern. The little cat jumped off the table, a slight whoosh escaping from him as he landed a little hard in his tiredness. He trotted over to the woman, though, eyes slightly squinted in anticipation of her soft and gentle hands. She reached down, wrapping the towel around him before lifting him to her lap. The purr rose within the little cat's chest as he pushed into her tummy while she tried to rub him dry. The wonderful chuckle sounded through the barn as the old woman shook her head at the little cat.

"And how do you expect me to rub this mud off you if you push yourself into me like that?" she laughed, gently lifting him away and cleaning along his back and sides. "I did miss you so, little fella. I'm so glad you're back," she said, not waiting to finish wiping him before holding him up against her cheek, cuddling him gently. As the little cat's purr increased, the dog moved from her spot and sat down at the woman's feet, resting her chin in the woman's lap. Such warmth!

"Ah, we could sit like this forever, couldn't we?" said the old woman, "but there's still plenty of cleaning to do before I can get you some food, so we'd better move on." She lowered the little cat, putting him down beside the dog's face and continuing her wiping.

"Oh, Blue," she cried, as she began to wipe his tail, "you've hurt yourself!" Carefully, she drew the towel along his tail, stopping just below the bend. "Poor, brave fellow. Something bit you, didn't it? This looks nasty. I'll have to clean it up a little, though; it's got mud in it. I'll get some of that disinfectant I use for the horses; there's no telling where you've been, who bit you or what's in this muck."

She patted the dog's head, urging her to move it, then gently lifted the little cat and returned to the table. Putting him down, she went to the shelf, opened a sealed container and took out some clean gauze and a bottle. "You can hold real still, can't you, little fella?" she said as she returned. "I'll be as gentle as I can, but it might sting a little. Good thing you are such a brave fellow. Come on."

She soaked some gauze with the disinfectant before lifting Blue gently and tucking him securely under her left arm. She poured a little disinfectant right onto his tail to take the worst of the dirt off before gently dabbing the end with the soaked gauze. The little cat didn't move, though his eyes were wide, very wide. The barn was strangely quiet as the woman dabbed and dabbed, cleaning the dirt from the raw, bald spot at the tip of the tail. The little dog moved close, stretching her head toward the head of the little cat and gently licking his face. "That's a girl," said the woman, "you help us out here."

Satisfied that she'd done the best she could, the woman patted the sore spot with a clean, dry piece of gauze and held the little cat up against her cheek again. "There you are, little guy. It looks nasty, but it's clean now. I'll call the Doc in the morning and have him look at you. We'll have to have this dog checked too. Maybe he'll know who she belongs to. You know we can't keep her if she belongs to someone else, though Lord knows whoever it is ought to be tanned for such neglect! Meanwhile, we'll look after her, won't we, Blue?" she crooned as she rubbed her face against the little tabby head. Despite his stinging tail, the little cat began to purr loudly. Again, the dog padded in close, leaning against the woman and looking up at them, her tail wagging.

"Alright," the woman said, lowering the cat, "we've more work to do. You'll do for now, Blue. I can dry you some more when we go inside, but first I have to work a little more on this dog. She'll chill if I don't get her cleaner than she is."

Both animals wondered how anybody could chill around such a warm woman, but Blue happily washed his ears with his right paw as usual while the dog rolled over to let the woman tend to her matted hair. After using some of the horse brushes to clean the worst of the mud from the dog and begin to untangle the matted fur, the woman gave the dog a good rub with the towel she had used for the cat. When she was done, the dog stood up and shook herself violently, liking the feel of untangled hair. Chuckling again, the woman said, "Just you wait until we have you properly cleaned. Then you'll know what a really good shake is." The dog's tail thumped loudly against the floor.

Quickly the woman cleaned up the mess they'd made in the barn, taking the soiled hay out to the waste pit, carefully replacing the antiseptic and then sweeping the floor. "Time for some food," she said, as she put out one lantern and then the other; "Come on."

The little cat trotted over to the door and stepped outside, stopping to wait, the dog following his every move. The old woman closed the barn doors, saying, "Good night, horses. Good night, little donkey. We'll see you in the morning." As she turned toward the house, the little cat took up his place by her left leg, trotting eagerly at her side, and the dog followed close behind.

CHAPTER NINETEEN

FED

"Looking forward to some kibbles, Blue?" she asked as the three of them walked along the path to the verandah. "I think you'd better have some warm milk tonight, too. This dog looks like she could use some milk as well. I'll heat hers tonight too, for you've both been wet and chilled to the bone. Besides, she's got no meat on her to keep her warm. She looks like she's never been inside, though, so I'll have to fix her a spot on the verandah. Never did know an outside dog who was comfortable in the house. Still, I'll leave it up to her. I'm sure she'll make her own choice."

Sure enough, at the door to the house, the dog stopped. Blue went in, eager for his milk and food, and the woman went in behind him. The dog sat down outside the door. The woman turned and said, "Do you want to come in, pooch? It's okay for tonight, warm and dry in here, you know." She stood aside, holding the door open. The dog didn't move. The little cat took up his place beside the woman and looked at the dog, and the woman patted her thigh gently, urging the dog to join them. In response, the dog lay down in the doorway. "Okay, old girl; I'll fix you some milk and something to eat and bring it out to you," said the woman as she softly closed the door.

Inside, the woman quickly stoked the fire, put the kettle and some milk on to heat. Blue trotted over to his dish of kibbles and immediately settled down to eat. He was hungry! The woman went to a shelf in the pantry and found old Rex's feed dish and water bowls. She put a small amount of her own soup into the feed dish, filled one bowl with water and left the other for the milk. While she waited for things to heat up, she rummaged around in the storage room, finally coming out with a tattered old sweater and some ragged scarves. "I'll make the dog a bed of these. She'll be comfortable and safe out there, Blue."

When the woman opened the door, the dog sat up eagerly,

already happy in this new place. The woman rubbed the shaggy head and scratched behind her ears before arranging the old woolies on the floor beside the door. "You can have Rex's spot, doggy," she said; "it's dry and sheltered. You'll be just fine here as soon as you get some food. Can't give you too much tonight, though; it looks like you haven't eaten a good meal for ages. Have to be a bit careful."

The dog sniffed the woolies and stepped onto them, sitting down happily, head tilted to one side as she looked at this new friend. "I'll be right back," she said. Eager, the dog stood up and moved right in front of the door, tail half wagging.

Inside, the woman deftly made a pot of tea and set it on the warming shelf before pouring the warmed milk into the saucer for the little cat and the empty bowl for the dog. When she put the saucer of warm milk down on the cat's little mat, he immediately moved from his kibbles and settled in front of the saucer, lapping quickly. "That a boy, Blue," she said, turning back to the other dishes, "you've earned a good meal."

Thinking about the thin dog outside, she decided to add some bread to the soup, hoping that would help satisfy her and soothe any shock food would give to her system. The bread swelled, soaking up the good broth and filling out the soup. "That should help her," the woman said aloud, as she headed toward the door. Opening it, she was immediately greeted by the dog, waiting intently. Her tail thumped a few times.

"Here you go," said the woman, as she placed the bowl of milk down first. "You take it easy now and lap this up slowly while I get your food and water." The dog thrust her head into the bowl and lapped noisily. The woman chuckled. "I had almost forgotten how noisy you mutts are when you eat. The cat barely makes a sound and the horses are quiet when they suck their water up, but you dogs make a racket and a mess."

So happy was the dog to have her own dish of milk, she carried on slurping up the milk, oblivious to the woman's words. Though the woman had cautiously given only a small portion of milk, the

dog couldn't remember having had so much at once and she could-
n't believe her good fortune. She felt warm all over as she licked
the bottom of the bowl dry and she held her tail higher than usual
as she lifted her head, a few drops of milk dripping from her lips. If
she hadn't been so tired, she thought she might run around for
sheer joy. Instead, she started toward the woolies the woman had
put down. They were nice: soft, warm and smelling wonderfully
like the gentle woman herself.

Just as the dog settled down ready to tuck her nose under her
back feet and go to sleep, she heard the woman's steps coming back
to the door. Quickly she got up, meeting the woman as she opened
the door. "Your eyes look a little brighter already, pooch. Was that
good?" she asked with a soft smile. The dog wagged her tail vigorously and tipped her head slightly to the right as she gazed up into
the woman's face. "You don't even realize I have more for you, do
you?" asked the woman with another chuckle. "Poor thing. Well,
I do. I'm sorry I don't have any kibbles, but I've fixed up some of
my soup for you. That will have to do for now," she said, bending
to set the food dish and the full water dish down on the verandah.

Catching the delicious scent of the food and seeing the woman
put it down for her, the dog quivered all over as she moved to the
dishes and again thrust her head into the bowl, suddenly aware of
nothing but the contents of the dish. Never had she eaten anything
so wonderful! Never had she eaten so much at one time so easily.
This food had no feathers to spit out, no fur to tear away; it was just
food, all ready to eat. Hungrily, the dog chomped up the meal,
once again licking every last bit from the bowl. Oh, this was wonderful!

The old woman chuckled again as the dog raised her head from
the empty bowl, a look of deep satisfaction in her dark brown eyes.
She licked her lips twice and sat down, still gazing at the wonderful
woman. Her tail thumped hard against the verandah floor as the
woman bent over, patted her head and gave her a good scratch
behind the ear. In pure pleasure, the dog bent slightly to the side
and scratched wildly at her neck with her hind leg, joining the

woman's gentle ear-scratches. "Good dog," said the woman, returning to patting the shaggy head softly. "You settle into your bed for
the night now. I'll peek out at you before I go to bed, but you'll be
just fine here. Have a good sleep."

As the woman closed the door softly behind her, the dog
stepped onto the soft woolies, turned around until she was just
right, then tucked her head beneath her back paws. With a huge
sigh of contentment, she soon drifted off to sleep, more warm, dry
and comfortable than ever in her life. Inside, the woman poured
herself a cup of tea and took it to the rocker by the stove. Blue, having finished his meal and his milk, began to purr even as he walked
across the floor to hop up on her lap. He, too, turned around until
he found just the right place before curling into a ball on the soft
lap. Never had his purr been louder or sweeter than in those
moments as he tucked himself up against the soft tummy and the
chair began to rock gently. His eyelids fell almost shut as he gave
himself up to the warmth and comfort of his safe place.

"Oh, Blue," said the old woman, "this is nearly perfect. I haven't
felt quite this safe since old Rex left us. Did you know that, little
fella? Did you go to get the black dog just to fill in that gap, to help
us out? You are a clever and brave little fellow, aren't you? You did
a fine job. We'll just check with Doc in the morning. While we
wait for him, we'll have to do some more cleaning. Poor dog has
been badly neglected, but she's not the least wild or angry, is she?
Does she need us too, Blue?"

As she gently rocked the chair, sipping tea with one hand and
evenly stroking the little cat with the other, she continued her chat-
tering, though she soon knew the weary cat had gone to sleep.
"Poor little fellow; you're all tired out, aren't you? Well, I'll just finish my tea and then we'll go to bed. It was a long, long day for me,
too, worrying about you, but it has all come out well. I should have
known it would with such a fine cat as you, my little Blue come
home to stay."

CHAPTER TWENTY

GOOD MORNING

Despite her eagerness to call the vet in the morning and continue cleaning up the dog and cat, the old woman slept in. Neither
the little cat nor the black dog stirred early to waken her, all three
having slept more soundly than they could recall. The little cat lifted his little head from his soft, warm pillow only when he heard the
woman exclaim, "Gracious, Blue, look how long we've slept!"
Then, with a yawn and a stretch, he hopped down from the bed and
took up his place by the woman's side as she began her day, dress-
ing and making the bed.

The dog, warm and secure and with a full belly, wakened only
when she heard the pad of the woman's feet going into the kitchen.
She, too, yawned and stretched, then gave a mighty shake. Oh, how
good she felt! Seeing the little cat sitting on the window sill, looking out at her, the dog gave a wag of her tail before leaping down
the verandah steps and having a quick tear around the yard, giving
herself up to her new sense of the joy of life. Though she had no
expectations and no demands to make, the dog hurried back to the
verandah, simply eager to please and to give. Life was good, and she
wanted to share!

Inside, the little cat divided his attention between watching the
dog move about so happily and watching the woman go about her
morning chores. As she built up the fire and prepared the breakfast
things, the woman hummed a while before bursting into full song.
"All things bright and beautiful, all creatures great and small; all
things wise and wonderful; the Lord God made them all," sang the
gentle voice as the woman moved over to the phone on the wall.

"Oh, Doc; it's Martha again. I need you to come out to the old
farm. No, nothing too urgent or serious; it's my little cat mostly.
Something has taken a chunk out of his tail; looks like it's broken
too. He was hurt going to bring a sorry-looking dog home. I need
you to have a look at her, too. Maybe you'll know whose she is and

79

what I should do with her. No, no; she's as gentle and kind as can be, though she's been neglected. Later this morning? That will be just fine; it will give me a chance to clean the dog up some more so you can have a better look at her. Good thing it's a fine day. Thanks ever so much, Doc. See you later."

Turning back to the stove, the woman quickly arranged the kettle and pot so they would simmer gently while she hurried out to give the horses some feed. "C'mon, Blue," she said, "we're a lazy and late bunch this morning and we must feed the horses before we eat ourselves. Besides, we have lots to do this morning."

The little cat hopped down from the window sill and hurried after the old woman, pausing patiently at the door as she put on her warm jacket and shoes. The dog, hearing footsteps just inside the door, sat herself down facing the door, tail wagging eagerly. As the door opened, she let out a delighted "woof" before hopping around in tight circles in her happiness to see the kind woman and little cat. The wonderful chuckle rang out across the morning air as the woman reached down and rubbed the shaggy black head.

"And good morning to you too, pooch," she laughed. "You're as funny as this little cat. Had a good sleep, did you? Ah, but you're as lazy as we are this morning. Don't you think you can sleep your life away." The black dog was so excited by such a warm greeting, her tail wagged so hard it turned right in circles like a helicopter blade rotating over her back. Again, the rich chuckle rang out. Hearing it, the little cat had to join in; his rich purr added to the morning song as he rubbed back and forth against the good woman's legs.

With a few more pats on the dog's head and a scratch behind the little cat's ear, the woman turned and went down the stairs. As always, the cat took up his position by her left leg, but the dog was so overjoyed, she had to run in large circles, tail wagging, ears blowing out behind her as she ran. As the woman and cat made their straight path to the barn, the dog looped her way along, drawing next to them every few yards before making her next loop. She stopped her circling only as they entered the barn, though she was still clearly excited.

Nose bent to the ground, she quickly sniffed her way around the barn, scurrying into corners and down the alley, pausing before each stall door for extra sniffs, snorting a little as she investigated. At each stall, a large head peered over the door and bent down a little to investigate in return and at each stall, brown eye met brown eye for a moment as the assessment process began. Initial conclusions being favourable, the dog hurried on with her investigation, enjoying the brightness and cleanness of this new barn. And the hay that the woman was tossing into the stalls! So clean, so fresh. Another low "woof" escaped the dog's throat as she turned a few tight circles in the alley before trotting outside for a few more romps around the yard.

"Oh, Blue," laughed the woman, "what a bundle of energy she is this morning. Have you ever seen anything like it? Goodness knows what she'll be like when she has been cared for properly, that is if we get to care for her, of course. Never mind, we've done her some good already."

'No, I've never seen anything like it,' thought the little cat. 'If you only knew how miserable life was for her before, you'd know just how much good. Still, she is a little carried away. You'd never see me acting such a fool over some love. No, not me. She's a good dog and a nice friend, but she could use a little dignifying,' he concluded as he gave his face a good wash while waiting for the woman to finish.

When the woman and cat headed back to the house, the dog joined them, trotting on the other side of the woman, head raised to look into the kind face as they walked along. The woman noted the bit of a glint in the gentle brown eyes as the dog soaked up each moment of happiness. "Do you know you're going to get another meal?" she asked. "I don't think so, somehow. Well, you are. I'll have to give you a couple of small meals for a few days before swinging you over to one larger one. That is, if you can stay. If you do, before long, you'll be as improved as little Blue is. When he came, his coat was kind of dull, and he tired easily. Now, he's as glossy and handsome as can be and he's ever so strong. Look how well he came through yesterday!"

After slurping up her milk and licking her bowl of soup so clean it looked as if the dish had been washed, the dog returned to her woolie bed and napped while the woman and cat took their breakfast inside. "Come on, Blue; just my tea to drink now. There's always time for a little cuddle before we move on to the chores," she said as she pushed her bowl back and patted her lap. Blue left his little mat and deftly hopped up, purring as he settled into his comfy place there.

"You're the best puss in the world," she said, stroking him carefully. "The dog may take some extra time this morning while I try to clean her up, and I love her too already, but nobody takes the place of my little cat come home to stay. You'll help me when I bath her, won't you, Blue? I don't know how she'll like the water, and she'll feel better if you're around. She seems to know you well. I wonder what you two know that I don't? Guess, I'll never know. Doesn't matter, though. Right now we have a job to do."

Blue hopped onto the window sill to watch the day and the woman as the woman tidied the kitchen and rummaged around in the storage room. When she came out, she had a pail, soap, soft rags and some old towels as well as a comb and brush. "These belonged to old Rex," she said; "they ought to do the trick for black dog. We'll get to the job as soon as we turn the horses out. I hate leaving the barn chores until later, but I do want to clean the dog up before the Doc comes, so we'll just do things a little backwards this morning. Nice that it doesn't matter, isn't it?"

As the woman got her coat on again, Blue stretched and jumped down to join her. Hearing them, the dog also rose and stretched before facing the door, tail wagging as she wondered what was next. Her tail wound round and round again when the door opened and she saw the good friends, but this time she trotted happily along with them to the barn.

"We have to let the horses out, now," said the woman. "Isn't this wonderful, Blue? You can sit up on the rafters somewhere and not have to worry. I just know this dog will help out. She's so giving."

Sure enough, the dog stayed close beside the woman when Blue scampered up onto a beam above old Sarah's stall. Uncertain but not afraid, the dog cocked her head to one side and looked up at the woman as she opened Fawn's stall door. As the old horse paused for her morning rub, the dog sat absolutely still, looking intently at the horse, ready to defend the gentle woman against this big beast if necessary. As the woman talked softly to the horse and rubbed her gently, the dog relaxed a little, sensing no danger at all. Before moving on out of the barn, Fawn bent her head down to the dog, paused unmoving for a moment, then swung around and moved steadily into the morning air, the dog following along at her side as far as the barn door where she sat and watched as the horse walked away.

The dog repeated her performance as each horse was turned out, then met old Sarah. The little donkey was much closer to the dog's size than the horses were and they eyed each other cautiously. The gentle woman put one hand down on the dog's head as she stroked Sarah's long ears. "Sarah's different, pooch. She stays in a while. I'll have to do the water buckets now or she won't go out. You don't have to marshal her out and you don't have to worry that she'll hurt me. She just needs love like everyone else," she said, as she rubbed dog and mule together before stepping back and moving to the water hose.

Brown eye looked into brown eye for quite a while before the assessment was complete and the dog moved around the donkey to see what the woman was doing. It was also time for the little cat to hop down and play with the hose, so soon gentle woman, donkey, dog and cat all moved about the bright barn, enjoying the morning together.

CHAPTER TWENTY-ONE

A BATH

As usual, when the woman finished the water buckets, the little donkey came for another rub on the nose and stroke on the ears before turning and heading for the pasture. The cat hopped and pounced as the woman rolled up the hose, and the dog sat, head tipped to one side, wondering what kind of game that was. Seeing the fun, she decided to join in. As the cat sprang lightly onto the hose and clasped it between two paws, the dog jumped at the end, grabbed the nozzle in her mouth and pulled. Immediately, the hose began to unwind. The woman couldn't help but laugh loudly before calling, "No, pooch!" and grabbing the handle of the reel to prevent the hose running out any further. "We have to wind it up, pup. This is not a game for dogs." Black dog trotted quickly over to the woman's side, pawing the air with one front leg while hanging her head slightly.

"It's okay, pooch," said the woman, as she took the paw in one hand and patted the head with another. "You were just playing, weren't you? You're a good dog." Reassured, the dog settled down to watch as the woman rewound the hose and the little cat resumed his game, pouncing and grabbing ever so lightly. She also watched her pour something into a bucket and fill it with water, great foamy bubbles rising to the top of the pail as it filled. "This is for you, pooch," she said; "we're going outside for a bath. I'd better change my jacket first, though. I'll slip this old raincoat of Josiah's on before we go out."

Into the large pockets of the long coat, she slipped some scissors, a curry comb and a wire comb before calling the dog, picking up the pail and moving outside. "You come too, Blue. You can at least watch." The dog trotted along at the woman's side as they moved into a sunny spot over by the house. The little cat walked along behind, a little unsure of the foamy bucket. When the old woman put it down near the tap that came out of the house, he cautiously stood up resting one front foot on the rim of the bucket, ears erect, whiskers atwitch. With his other front paw, he reached out very tentatively and took a cautious swipe at the white foam. Instantly, he dropped to the ground, frantically flicking his paw and shaking his head. Bubbles again!

Whiskers flicking, he loped away to the stump near the verandah where he sat licking the slippery mess from his paw. The great chuckle rose from the good woman as she watched him. "Don't worry, little fella," she laughed; "this stuff is not for you. It's for the dog. I won't wet you, fussy puss." The cat just continued his important cleaning.

"Are you ready, pooch?" she asked. "Hope you like water because I'm going to hose you a bit before I start scrubbing." The dog looked up at her, head tipped to one side, tongue sticking out one side of her mouth, tail wagging happily. The old woman placed one hand on the dog's neck before she turned the hose on gently and began to soak the black coat. Immediately, the dog shook, sending water everywhere. Again, the old woman laughed. "Can't bother me, pooch. I've got this fine coat on, so shake away!" she chuckled as she hosed and rubbed the unruly coat.

The little cat drew further back on his stump to be sure he would be out of reach of the flying water drops. He wrinkled his nose slightly as an unpleasant smell drifted his way, causing him to switch from washing his paw to washing his face, rubbing quite hard with his right paw as always. He had a lot of scrubbing to do this morning.

The old woman couldn't help but wrinkle her nose up a bit too as the water began to loosen some of the muck that had been caked on the dog, but she talked cheerfully as she held the dog with one hand while rubbing her all over with a cloth soaked in the soapy water. "Ach, pooch," she said, "you've been in some wretched places haven't you? Never mind. I'll just scrub and clip until you're all clean. That's it, you stand still while I work on you. You don't mind the water, do you? Must have some Lab in you. What a sight you are now, though, all wet and soapy, muddy water running from your belly and down your legs. And look how your hair stands straight up all over your head!" The great chuckle rang out accompanied by the sounds of the dog shaking and water flying. She scrubbed and scrubbed, then scrubbed some more before turning the hose back on to begin rinsing. "I should have put a rain hat on too," she laughed, as the dog sent a wall of water right up onto her face and hair. Still she carried on, rinsing and rubbing until the bubbles were gone, and the foul smell was replaced by the much cleaner but heavy smell of wet dog.

"Not done yet," she said as she turned off the hose, still keeping one hand on the dog's neck so she wouldn't run off. Quickly she turned her back as the dog gave another great shake, water drops flying far and near and running off the long raincoat and the side of the house. "Black dog, you are a sight to behold!" she said, giving way to great peals of laughter. "I've never seen anything quite like that hair on your head. Why it stands straight up when it's wet. All the rest of you waves and curls but you've a topnotch like a rooster on your head. Funny pooch!" Sensing the warmth and joy in the woman's voice, the dog just looked up and wagged her tail, sending more water spraying about.

"Come on," said the woman, "I'm going to rub you as dry as I can now so I can see what kind of tangles and mess you have on your legs and belly. Come away from all this water to the towels I brought out." The dog trotted beside her, head tipped and looking up into the kind old face. "Can you sit?" she asked when they reached the grass by the path. "Good dog. I knew you were smart," she crooned as she began to rub the black dog vigorously with the old towels. The wet tail thumped against the grass as she worked. Finally, she gave even the tail a good scrub before putting some old but clean burlap sacks on the ground and having the dog lie down on them. "That's it, girl; you roll over so I can rub your belly," she said, gently patting the side of the dog's neck before beginning her task.

She knelt beside the dog and rubbed and combed the hair on her belly and legs. Several times she had to stop and clip away

matted bits with her scissors. Always she talked soothingly to the
dog as she worked, quick to pause when she saw any wincing at all.
In some places, the hair had been so matted that the skin was
rubbed sore underneath, so the woman worked carefully. As she
combed and clipped the dog lay still, eyes half shut in a kind of
warmth she had never known.

Seeing the water-fight part was over, the little cat soon joined
them, taking his place beside the woman. She paused long enough
in her work to give the little cat head a scratch, saying, "Good puss.
Aren't you happy you never had such dirt as this? Poor dog has been
carrying muck around for goodness knows how long. Dogs just
aren't clean like you little pusses are but they shouldn't be left this
dirty either."

"I think that's it, pooch," she said, stretching her back after stooping so long. "Up you get so I can give you a quick brush all over."
The dog squirmed onto its tummy and sat up, giving another shake
even as she sat. No water flew this time! Quickly but gently the
woman brushed the dog's head, ears and back, running one gentle
hand along after the quick brush strokes. "We'll have to fatten you
up a bit, pooch," she said. "You're all skin and bones under this
thick coat. Guess you must have your winter coat already. Well, it
will soon be here. Good thing you are ready."

The dog shuddered in delight at the soft touch and attention.
Finally the woman combed the thick tail before turning her
attention to the dog's ears and face. With a soft, damp cloth, she
very carefully wiped the dog's eyes, nose and then the inside of
the floppy ears. "You've even got some mud stuck in here, miss.
I'll have to rub them with a bit of mineral oil. You wait here while
I get some."

The dog shook herself a few times before sitting down on the
sacks to wait as the woman hurried off to the sealed container in the
barn. Coming back she exclaimed, "What a good pup. Smart as a
whip!" The tail thumped the ground and the black head, still a
little fuzzy on top, tipped again to one side as the brown eyes
glowed at the good woman. Kneeling again beside the patient

dog, the woman deftly tended to the ears, cleaning them carefully before rubbing the mineral oil into the soft folds.

"There now," she said, "you may not win any ribbons at a show but you're a perfectly respectable pooch now!" The dog let a low "woof" roll from her throat as she swished her tail back and forth before giving another shake. The wonderful chuckle burst from the kind woman once more as she said, "Didn't I say you'd love a good shake when you were really clean? Good dog." Even the little cat moved closer to show his approval of the transformed dog, purring as he rubbed against the dog's clean front legs.

Suddenly the woman burst into loud laughter as she stood up straight. Looking down at the clean dog and the clean cat, her eyes crinkled in delight as she exclaimed, "Now look who is the dirty one. You're both fit to show, and here I am in this dirty old raincoat with my hair dripping down my back. I must be a sight to behold now!" She continued to laugh and chuckle as she scratched the chin of the clean black dog and the ear of the clean tabby cat. "My turn to clean. You two stay here in the sun while I put the things away and tidy myself up before Doc gets here."

As the old woman went about her chores, the dog lay back down on the sacks, head up so she could watch the woman. The little cat, with a few happy meows, stepped onto the sack next to the dog and sat down, squeezing his eyes up in pleasure as he leaned slightly against the dog's leg. As the two old friends sat in the morning sun, watching the woman rinsing the cloths and the pail and putting things away, the little cat thought about how much better it was sitting here with the good dog than it had been crouched down, hiding behind the dirty barn of the old place. He couldn't stop the low purr from erupting. The clean dog sighed in complete agreement and rested her chin on her front paws.

CHAPTER TWENTY-TWO

TO STAY

The little cat curled into a ball next to the dog and dozed off in the morning sun, though there wasn't a lot of warmth left in it so late in the fall. The woman hummed contentedly as she changed from the wet raincoat back to her warm jacket and tidied herself up. She had barely finished toweling, combing and rebraiding her hair when she heard the old van rattling down the drive. Immediately, the dog and cat sat erect, a series of loud barks exploding from the dog. Ears flat and legs bent keeping his body close to the ground, the little cat immediately ran over to the woman and wound himself about her legs. The dog, barking sharply, trotted toward the van, eyes fixed on its driver.

"Come here, pooch," called the woman as she bent and scooped the little cat into her arms. "It's okay. Come on. Good girl. Now sit," she said, firmly but gently. Only a little reluctantly, the dog sat beside the woman and little cat, a low growl rumbling in her throat punctuated by the occasional low bark, despite the gentle hand resting on her head.

"Good morning, Doc," Martha called cheerfully as an older version of Allan got out of the van and walked toward them. He was tall and sturdily built and his tanned face was softened by deep laugh lines around his bright but kind blue eyes. His thick hair was peppered with grey and a few unruly tufts hung down across his forehead. His sturdy boots thudded slightly as he strode confidently along, and his deep blue coveralls rustled slightly as he walked. The little cat drew as close to the woman's body as he could, glad of her safe arm holding him. The dog also drew closer as she eyed the big man carefully, every muscle in her body tense, the low rumble continuing in her throat.

"Mornin' Mrs. Oaks. Is this to be a welcoming party or a guard patrol? It's a beautiful sight, whichever it is," he said with obvious delight in his deep, musical voice. He stopped a few feet away and knelt on one knee. "Introduce me to these fine friends of yours," he said, settling comfortably on his heel and resting his big hands on his knee.

Mrs. Oaks moved over beside him, the dog staying close at her side, quiet now, and the little cat pressed into her tummy. "Sit, pooch," she said, dropping her hand onto her head. "Good dog."

"Well, Doc. Good to see you. This is Blue, my little cat come home to stay. Blue, this is Doc, a good friend," she said gently while rubbing Blue softly with her fingers. Doc waited while Blue gazed at him, nose twitching, tail flicking slowly.

"Hello, little fella," said Doc, "hear you've had a rough day. What a pretty puss. You're like me, tabby but really more speckled grey than anything aren't you? I didn't used to be tabby, mind you. No, I was once all one colour. You cats are born good looking though, aren't you?"

As he kept up his soothing talk, the Doc gently offered the back of his hand to the little cat. Blue reached his head further forward, sniffing, ears erect. He smelled many familiar things: dogs, cats, horses, cows, even some grass. He also got a whiff of something like what was on the end of his own tail now. Nothing smelled dirty here, and this voice was much more like the kind woman than like the rough men he had known before. Relaxing a little, Blue looked into the bright eyes, his own eyes squinted slightly. Assured, he reached out one paw and placed it on the big, brown hand.

"That's it, little fella; come on over here, then," said the Doc as the woman lowered the cat onto his knee. "Let's have a look at that tail. Oh, you've had a bite alright, haven't you? Taken a good hunk of fur and broken the end. Bet that hurts a lot. Hold still while I just feel this crook; that a boy. Good puss." The little cat held perfectly still while the man felt his tail and moved on to examine his body and head, checking the little ears and looking at his teeth.

"Good boy," he said, handing him back to Mrs. Oaks. "He'll be fine. His tail is broken but it's best left alone to heal. It will probably be crooked but that won't hurt him. I think most of the fur will grow back in, too, and you've got that slash nice and clean, so I'll leave it too. He's a clean cat and will tend to it himself. He's also in good health and strong. Allan was right when he told me he was a grand fellow."

"Oh, thanks, Doc. I love him to bits, and it's been so much easier having him here. What do you make of this ragamuffin he brought home? I've spent all morning cleaning her up. She's a real good pup, just starved for love, I think," she said, scratching the dog behind the ear. The shaggy black head tipped slightly to the side and brown eyes gazed up at the good woman, a hint of a question in them. "It's okay, pooch; you saw he was good to Blue. He's just fine. That a girl. You sit still while he has a look."

Once again, the vet offered the back of his hand. The damp, black nose rubbed against it, sniffing rapidly. The dog stood up, tail giving a couple of half wags as she moved over to sniff more of the man. His coveralls smelled good, and his boots smelled more like this nice new barn than like the old one. She gave a few more wags as she continued her investigation, pausing only to look up briefly when she felt the large hand rest on her head. Slowly the vet patted her head and rubbed her neck before giving her a strong scratch behind the ears. That did it! She wagged her tail vigorously and looked up into the kind face.

"Good girl," he said, as he began to check her over. "Poor thing hasn't had a lot of food has she?" he asked, as he ran his hand over the sharp ribs. "She's a good sound dog, though. Nothing wrong that food and care won't cure in no time. I figured you'd need food, so I brought a sack out for you. Can't have her eating all your soup! Her eyes are clear and bright, aren't they? Yes, that's a good dog. Come on. Roll over so I can look at your belly."

The big dog flopped over at his feet, secure in his obvious care. "You've done a good job here, Mrs. Oaks. Looks like she never saw a comb until you fixed her up. I'll give you a little salve for these raw spots on her skin, but with proper care of her coat, those will just clear up. The salve will make it a little quicker and easier for the dog. You've even taken care of her ears, I see. That's just fine."

The vet gave the dog a few solid pats before standing up. "Come on, girl; up you get. That's it," he said as the dog rose and gave herself a good shake. "Off you go, now. I want to see you run a bit."

But the dog just stood between the old woman and the vet, looking happily from one face to the other, tail wagging, eyes glowing. Then she nudged the little cat with her nose. The happy chuckle rose from the woman's throat again and rang out across the farmyard. The vet's deep laughter joined and the dog gave a quick woof. "What a crew you've got now, Mrs. Oaks. You won't be lonely any more."

Putting the little cat down on the ground, she turned to look up at the kind vet, a little frown lining her brow and something clouding her eyes. "I don't know, Doc. I can't keep a dog that belongs to someone else. I kind of hoped you'd know if there'd been a stray around or if she belongs to someone or what. I don't know where the cat came from either, but he has made his choice. Somehow, I know that one is alright. The dog seems like an answer to prayer, but I wish I could be sure she's not someone else's."

At the concern in the good woman's voice, the little cat began to meow and rub against her legs. The dog moved closer to the woman, leaning slightly against her, and thumped her tail reassuringly on the ground. A great peal of laughter rolled from the vet and he threw his head back.

"They're yours alright," he said. "Look at them. I've never seen animals so loyal so fast. It's almost as if they read your mind. You say this little cat seemed to go off and fetch the dog for you? Looks to me like you haven't any choice anyway. This cat has chosen you and then brought the dog as a gift. It just isn't right to refuse a gift now is it?" Again the deep, rich laughter rang out.

This time, the woman joined him, though a little tentatively. "Are you sure, Doc? I'm afraid to get any more attached in case I have to give her up again."

"Animals know, Mrs. Oaks. They don't fool around like we do. They just know. If these two have come home to stay, then you'd best look after them. Besides, I have a hunch I know what's up here. Tell me, when this dog is all wet, does her hair stick up right funny like on her head? Does she have an unruly topnotch like I do?"

"Oh, yes she does. She's quite a sight — much more unruly than your few stray tufts. She looks like a great shaggy dog with a rooster's topnotch. The rest of her coat is just wavy and curly though."

The vet laughed again. "Then she's yours, Mrs. Oaks. I thought I recognized her. She used to have to scrounge for herself over at the old cow barn. They never wanted her over there, said she was no good and couldn't be trained. She was left to fend completely for herself. They won't miss her. Next time I'm there, though, I'll see to it that they don't bother you. My guess is the little cat might have come from there too. They've a barn full of cats they never bother with. They don't even feed them. It's a sad life they'll have had before they came here. If I'm not mistaken, I'd say you have some real good years ahead of you. I think these two are only about three years old and with the kind of care you give, they'll live a long while. You're a fine threesome now!"

As the Doc spoke, the cloud lifted from the old woman's face. Her eyes cleared and began to sparkle. The wrinkled face creased up as a huge smile spread across her face. In her relief, she laughed aloud, her head lifted in the bright sun. "Oh, Doc; that's the best news I've had for a long time," she bubbled as she bent down and threw her arms around the dog.

"You can stay, Rags. You can stay!" she cried, tears running down her face. "You may be an old ragamuffin, especially when you're wet, but I love you. I'm going to call you Rags, short for Ragamuffin, the best black dog around." With that she gave the shaggy head a good scratch before bending to scoop up the little cat.

"Oh, Blue," she cried. "You solved our barn problem didn't you? You're such a clever fellow. Thank you for bringing Rags home. We'll be just fine now, won't we? Just the three of us. Good puss."

The rich deep laughter of the vet rang across the fields as he looked at Blue, the little cat come home to stay, rubbing his head against the wrinkled cheek, great double purrs boiling from the kettle in his chest, and Rags, the solution to the problem, barking and leaping in tight circles around the feet of her good, old woman. It would be a wonderful winter on the old farm.

Québec, Canada
2000